MW00568390

Long Point

LAST PORT OF CALL

Long Point

— LAST PORT OF CALL —

Dave Stone

Stoddart

A BOSTON MILLS PRESS BOOK

Canadian Cataloguing in Publication Data

Stone, Dave, 1923-
    Long Point : last port of call

ISBN 0-919783-59-7

1. Shipwrecks - Ontario - Long Point (Haldimand-
Norfolk).   I. Title.

G525.S85 1988   363.1'23'0971336   C88-094016-6

FRONT COVER:
*The remains of one of Long Point's many victims fast aground
on the South Beach. — Dave Stone*

BACK COVER:
The Mystery Schooner of Long Point Bay. — John Veber

OVERLEAF:
*Boiler and boiler plate which assisted in the identification of the
Majestic. — John Veber*

*Note: "The Ghost Fleet of Long Point" chart is available at
21"x48".*

© David W. Stone, 1988.

Published in 1993 by   A BOSTON MILLS PRESS BOOK
Stoddart Publishing Co. Limited   The Boston Mills Press
34 Lesmill Road   132 Main Street
Toronto, Canada   Erin, Ontario
M3B 2T6   N0B 1T0
(416) 445-3333   (519) 833-2407

Design by Gill Stead
Printed at Ampersand, Guelph, Ontario

The publisher gratefully acknowledges the support of the Canada Council, Ontario
Ministry of Culture and Communications, Ontario Arts Council and Ontario
Publishing Centre in the development of writing and publishing in Canada.

Table of Contents

Foreword

I'd heard about David Stone long before I met him, but the day I strolled along the water's edge on Lake Erie's north shore with The Beachcomber and his dog Seaweed, I realized that I'd latched onto a truly colourful personality.

He didn't fit the usual beachcomber image. He didn't look like your typical old salt. He looked more like Fred Astaire, with the same mild-mannered charm and a mind as nimble as Astaire's tapping toes.

Earlier, when he had learned of my interest in doing an item about him for Global News, he had sent me a letter giving directions and whatnot to his place in Long Point. "I'll share with you my special kind of music," he wrote. "The sound of running waves, shifting sands and the wind in the weathered trees."

That did it! The following week my wife, Jenny, who's our production assistant, cameraman Terry Culbert and myself high-tailed it down to the Point to meet the man who for 35 years has studied the wrecks that lie asleep in the deep — which he charted in his now familiar map, "The Ghost Fleet of Long Point."

As I suspected, there's a lot of the poet in Beachcomber Stone. As we walked and talked I began to feel the romance and the tragedy of adventurous men pitted against hostile, treacherous waters. I could almost hear the howling winds and slashing waves that had tossed the ships like matchsticks towards the sandy shoals.

There's also a lot of the student in him. He researched. He read everything he could get his hands on about Great Lakes shipping. He sought out old seadogs, historians and divers. An experienced diver

The author with Bill Bramah at Long Point.

himself, he went down to get a first-hand look at some of the 160-odd wrecks and their historic artifacts so jealously hoarded by the lakes.

Later we went up to his lakefront cottage to meet his wife, Jean, his companion over the years of unflagging devotion to discovery. We listened as he spun tales of adventure and of his beloved Long Point.

In the following pages perhaps you'll become caught up, as we were, in the mysteries of the doomed ships that lie silently in the Graveyard of the Great Lakes.

Perhaps someday you too will have a chance to hear "the sound of running waves, shifting sands and the wind in the weathered trees." Or, in imagination, to walk with The Beachcomber and Seaweed along the water's edge of Lake Erie's north shore.

Bill Bramah
Global Television
November 1987

Acknowledgements

Many thanks are due to my friends for deciding that the time had come for me to write a book about Long Point, "The Graveyard of the Great Lakes." I could not have done it without the assistance of people like my friend the late Dr. Richard J. Wright, one of the most respected shipwreck researchers of his time, also Lorne Joyce, L. Stienstra, Doc Roher, John Veber, Tad Dickerson, Henry Daciuk, Harry Gamble, the late Ben Harris, the late Mrs. Lorne Brown, Julia Stone, William A. Fox, and K. William Hawkins, who also assisted in producing "The Ghost Fleet of Long Point."

Retired Long Point lighthouse keepers Bill Ansley, Clayton Schofield and Len Goodmurphy, along with the present keeper, Pat Kerr, also provided assistance.

I must also record my gratitude to the staff of the Canadian Wildlife Service for their co-operation over the years.

When I made the decision to write *Last Port of Call*, I could see the amount of work and the discipline required to accomplish this project. With all the research material I've collected and my personal experiences, I was sure I could come up with something.

A publisher was found by long-time friend and former Ingersoll resident Billie Gayfer Smith, now of Erin, Ontario. She too had been pushing me to write a book on Long Point and introduced me to The Boston Mills Press. John Denison, one of the partners of this publishing house, saw some of the material I had to offer and said, "Start writing." John, a former resident of Nanticoke on Lake Erie shores, was very familiar with Long Point.

With my material and a publisher lined up, I now had to decide where I was going to write the book. Starting off at my home in Ingersoll was no problem, but when I moved to the cottage at Long Point, I ran into much difficulty. There was no place to leave all the materials and no privacy — at Long Point there is always a procession of divers wanting to know where the wrecks are.

After about two weeks of this I decided to move back to Ingersoll, since I was accomplishing nothing. In desperation I went to the village of Port Rowan to see if I could rent a room. This really started the tongues wagging and rumours going. Why would Dave Stone be looking for another place to live? "Wife problems, I'll bet."

My wife, Jean, was telling a friend, Ted Buchanan, of my plight, and he immediately offered me a log cabin behind his property on the edge of the marsh, complete with a large grandfather frog to keep me company. This turned out to be an ideal place, plenty of solitude, with the exception of the wildlife in the marsh, and no visitors, as most people didn't know this cabin existed. For this, my thanks to Gail and Ted Buchanan.

Special praise goes to my wife, Jean, who ended up doing all the "man things" around the house due to my preoccupation. She also spent countless hours unscrambling my writings to make them readable.

This manuscript could not have been finished if it were not for Doreen Lawson, who typed this manuscript into a presentable form for the publisher.

Off these shores of Gravelly Bay many vessels have been sheltered from the ravages of the lake. However, these waters have also claimed more than one unwary vessel. — Dave Stone

Introduction

In writing this book, *Last Port of Call*, I hope to remind all those sailing today around this unique, lengthy sandspit of Long Point that at one time it was a deathtrap for many mariners. But I sincerely hope that the stories of this area's marine disasters do not frighten readers away from the waters off Long Point, Ontario. That is not the intention of this book.

This book is dedicated to the hundreds of people who lost their lives through shipwrecks on the Point. Many remain unidentified and lie in unmarked graves far from their native country. Some of these poor souls were the crews of vessels lost either during a violent storm or some other form of a disaster. Many more were passengers, mainly immigrants who had high expectations of finding a new life and carving out a homestead in this vast wilderness, only to have their lives and hopes dashed away forever on this treacherous sandy shoal called Long Point.

This book is also dedicated to the crew members of the Long Point lifesaving station. These men, from 1883 to the mid-1920s, risked their lives on many occasions to offer assistance and comfort to those in peril.

Also not to be forgotten are the lighthouse keepers who have kept the beacons flashing far onto the lake and the bay from 1830 to the present day. In the near future the Long Point lighthouse will become automated and the keepers' services will no longer be necessary.

These men left the comfort of their homes and, on a number of occasions, their families to serve mankind by making Long Point a safer place to travel. In the early years they received a low rate of pay for the dedicated function they performed. One can well imagine what the tally of shipwrecks and lives lost would be today if it were not for these responsible humanitarians.

Dave Stone
1987

The keeper's shanty on Second Island which I visited on my first trip to Long Point. High water cleaned this out a number of years ago.

My First Visit to Long Point

My fascination with Long Point began with my first visit in the summer of 1934. At that time my family had a cottage at Turkey Point and we spent the summers there. We did this for a number of summers until I joined the Royal Canadian Navy.

From where our cottage was located I could see the mysterious never-never land stretching out into the lake. The Point had few visitors, as in those days not many boats were available and some of the early out-boards were not too dependable.

I had heard stories about Long Point, and they all filled me with excitement. I knew I had to get out there. There were tales of shipwrecks, quicksand and bottomless bogs, murders, ghosts, skeletons lying on the beach and buried treasure. This was enough to arouse the curiosity and imagination of a young adventurer and make an impression that would last forever.

People used to refer to the Point as "The Forbidden Land." One Toronto newspaper published an article stating that there were more snakes per square mile on Long Point than there were in India. Large wampers supposedly hung from trees, waiting to seize an unwary visitor.

My first visit to the Point was made in an old wooden rowboat with an early Evinrude outboard, the gas tank for which was the size of a washtub. I also took a pair of oars and an extra five gallons of gas.

As I proceeded across the bay, and as Ryerson Island came closer and closer, my imagination ran wild. I didn't want to get too near to shore, as one of those large wampers might swim out and get me.

Eventually I arrived at the island. I could see large rope-like things going from tree to tree. Giant snakes. I immediately pointed the boat away from the beach and sped off at the wide-open speed of five miles per hour.

As I was distancing myself from shore, the motor started to sputter and then died. Despite numerous pulls on the starter cord, the old engine wouldn't even cough. With anxiety and a sore arm, I knew I was in trouble. What was I going to do? There were no boats in the area, my family had no idea where I was, and I had no food on board. I was going to be marooned on this land of evil reputation and would never be found.

The only thing I could do was to get out the oars and row ashore — and be prepared to face anything that might confront me.

The nearer I got to the white sandy beach, the more I wished I was home. I could see white bleached forms on the beach, twisted arms and fingers beckoning me to come nearer. I also saw objects which looked like bodies half buried in the sand.

The wind had begun to pick up, which it does nearly every afternoon, so I had to make land. I was too full of fear to get close to shore, so decided that I would row to the lighthouse, not realizing the great distance I was going to have to travel. My thinking was that once I got there I would get help and protection from the giant snakes.

I rowed to Second Island and there I spotted one of the keeper's shanties, well back from the beach, tucked under a large group of trees and covered with vines. The vines were my giant snakes. The skeletons and bodies were the bleached tree limbs and the half-buried logs.

I cautiously went ashore, still inspecting every place I put my foot down, and walked through the underbrush to the shanty. The door was unlocked, and when I entered, a small garter snake, which had been sleeping, left through the open door in disgust at being disturbed. This left me shaking in my boots, because I swore I saw rattles on the end of its tail.

I ran out of the cabin, shoved the boat offshore and rowed as fast as I could from that place. After rowing for about 20 minutes, I decided to give the motor another try. The first pull it coughed, the second it took off at full speed, nearly throwing me out of the boat. I didn't realize that the gas throttle was advanced to wide open. I picked myself up from the bottom of the boat, got things back in control again and headed for Turkey Point, realizing I would be safe as long as the motor kept going.

On my return trip I well imagined how Christopher Columbus had felt after he discovered America. My feelings had to be retained, as I couldn't tell anyone because I would be punished. I told my parents I was so late because I had been visiting a friend down the lake and had stayed too long. My biggest problem was how I was going to replace all the gas I had used on my trip to the Point. That was soon remedied by siphoning the necessary gas out of my father's car.

Little did I realize then that this was the beginning of a romance between myself and Long Point that would last a lifetime. It was just the first of many trips to this earthly Paradise.

The lighthouse standing like a giant memorial to all the ships that made Long Point their "Last Port of Call."
— Dave Stone

Shipwrecks

After the war and university I rented, then built, a cottage on Long Point and began spending summers there. With a 16-foot boat and outboard, I thought nothing of heading out to the lighthouse and then down to the south shore. I believe I spent more time out there that I did at my own cottage. The purpose of these trips was to look for evidence of old ships wrecked and washed up on the beach.

I had read stories of some of the wrecks that had occurred close to shore, but at this time there was very little research information available. I had to dig up my own facts. One piece of information that really excited me was a statement made by George Gamble of Port Dover: "When I came to Port Dover in 1922 there were still the hulls of 35 wrecks exposed on the Point."

Even before the turn of the century, if one went out to the tip of Long Point one could see the evidence of many marine disasters. Numerous masts and spars jutted up from the hulls of wrecked vessels. In fact, there were so many of them that they looked like a picket fence. To come around the Point and well down the south shore was a return trip of approximately 100 miles. At times the weather was more than threatening. It was a long trip home battling those heavy rollers.

To overcome this situation and to avoid becoming another wreck on this sandspit, a purchase was made. An American friend and I bought a leaky old boat which was in bad shape. However, after two weeks working on it, installing a new transom and using a gallon of caulking, we were ready for the launching. Now we could run down the south beach, and if there was any change in weather conditions, we could get home in short notice.

However, much to our dismay, there were several things that we had overlooked. The boat was so heavy that it took four men to drag it down to the beach every time it was used. It also leaked worse now than it did before we repaired it. But with one person bailing continuously and the other running the motor, we got along just fine.

On our one and only trip down the lake with this boat, we found part of the frame of a schooner. The excitement ran high, as we thought the rest of it must be nearby. Thoughts filled our heads of a valuable cargo; gold and priceless objects might be buried in the sand near the wreckage. We didn't realize then that the schooners of the 1800s and early 1900s were the workhorses of the Great Lakes, carrying cargoes such as grain, coal, lumber, salt, hides, stone and all the other commodities necessary for the early settlers to survive in this wilderness.

Looking at this piece of shipwreck lying on the beach raised many questions in my mind. What ship was this and what had happened?

Many years ago this piece of wreckage had been part of a sleek vessel in the launching ways. As she slipped into the water the builder stepped forward to admire his craftsmanship, very proud of his accomplishment. The owner, pleased with his investment, thought of the returns he would receive from transporting cargoes up and down the lakes. The captain, also present, a veteran Great Lakes sailor, found this vessel special. It was going to be his first command. Members of the crew were also nearby. Some were old sailors, very knowledgeable of the ways of the lakes, and for others it was their first time out. At a distant port, someone awaited the ship's cargo. No one could imagine on the day of the launch that the bones of this ship would soon be lying on the beach at Long Point.

We returned the leaky old boat to the party we had bought it from and didn't ask for our $50 back. In fact we didn't even charge him for the transom we had installed with great skill.

Standing on the beach at the end of Long Point, under a full moon, the only sound is that of gentle waves caressing the beach. Looking out into the lake, one can see the distant lights of a modern vessel working its way down to a designated port. All is well. Can this be Long Point, the Graveyard of the Great Lakes, the place whose name alone has struck terror in the hearts of all the men who have sailed these waters the past two centuries?

How quickly the scene changes — the pounding surf, the cold winds blowing with gale force, the cries of a shipwrecked sailor trying to save himself by clinging to a spar that has been torn loose from his stricken vessel by the raging storm. His cries will be to no avail. Even if he makes it to shore, his death will be by exposure. But his name will be added to the list of mariners who have made Long Point their "Last Port of Call."

The Point shows no preference in its victims, whether captain or crew, first-class passenger or steerage. Once they are in the cold, forbidding waters, neither their station in life nor their finery can save them from a watery grave.

This sickle-shaped peninsula stretches south and east from the mainland 32 kilometres into the middle of Lake Erie. Since man has been sailing the Great Lakes, the Point's long arm has been gathering unwary sailors, vessels and cargoes into its bosom. Eventually pieces of wreckage and bodies of crew members reach the white sandy beaches. There is no one to mourn those lost souls, and soon a shroud of sand covers and uncovers them at nature's whim. The only sound to disturb their rest is the wind in the weathered trees. Because of the fury of the late-fall storms, these bleached bones of lost ships have been showing up in the shallow water or on the beach for the past two centuries, and will continue to do so.

This book tells some of the stories of shipwrecks and other interesting happenings and folklore on Long Point. With the great number of ships that the Point has harvested over the past two centuries, it would take more than one book to tell the complete story. Current research indicates that there are approximately 175 to 200 vessels lost off Long Point.

A section of 59 Highway where ships used to sail through. This was once covered with water, being part of the Long Point Cut.

Long Point — Nautical Graveyard

When nature started building this sandspit 6,000 years ago, the water and land in this part of the world were of no concern to man, but the sandbars just off the shores were starting to form, getting into position to wreak destruction on ships of the distant future.

Long Point's beckoning arm stretches 32 kilometres out into the middle of Lake Erie, into its deepest depths. Because the peninsula extends halfway across the lake, it has to be avoided by mariners. The Point has narrowed their passageway across this body of water by about half.

Early sailors caught in violent waters or a fog, with no radio or radar to aid them, would often end up shipwrecked on the sandbars or the Point.

With all the sandbars around the Point reducing the passageway, traffic in the remaining open body of water was quite congested. As a result, there were a number of collisions.

The prevailing southwest winds also contributed to ship destruction and loss of life. Some of the smaller craft, carrying cargoes to the little ports along the lake, would navigate not too far off the shoreline. In fact sometimes they used the shoreline as a guide. They would try to stay just far enough away from the shoal's clutches. When caught in a southwest gale, these ships would be driven towards land and, with no turning room, end up fast aground, eventually to be pounded to pieces.

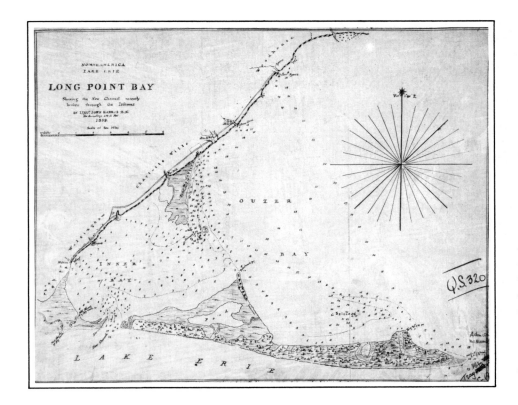

1838 chart of the Long Point Cut published according to Act of Parliament at the Hydrographic Office of the Admiralty, August 7, 1839. — Canadian Hydrographic Service, Environment Canada

Frequently, when a ship was in peril, the captain would try to sail around the tip of the Point. Accomplishing this, his vessel could ride out the storm in the shelter of the lee side. There they could stay, usually with a number of other vessels, until the blow settled down.

Prior to 1830 this feat was difficult, as there was no lighthouse to guide them around the end of the Point. In a fog this manoeuvre would sometimes prove disastrous. Thinking he had cleared the tip, the captain would change course and run the vessel aground, resulting in another unwary victim being claimed.

Modern sailors still seek shelter around the Point and in the outer bay. I have seen, on a number of occasions during foul weather, a dozen or more commer-cial ships riding out a storm. At night, with their lights on, it looks like a small town on the horizon.

Another hazard which trapped ships is the Bluff Bar. This is located in the outer bay, approximately four miles northeast from the lighthouse. The bar, which runs for three miles, has depths running from less than one foot to 20. This bar is ever changing, depending on the currents and wave action. Water levels are also a factor in assisting the bar to confuse the mariner. During high water some sections of the bar can be travelled over without problems. However, at low water levels, ships can run hard aground. During my lifetime I have seen this bar completely out of the water, looking like small sandy islands in the middle of nowhere.

Today's sailor has an advantage in avoiding this hazard. The bar is now well marked with a buoy at either end and is clearly defined on the charts.

Even with these advantages, Bluff Bar still traps those who are careless. Nearly every year a sailboat with a fixed keel gets caught and held fast by the clutching bar. Some, sailing too close to it and not watching their course, sail their craft right on it. Others anchor too near, the wind shifts slightly, and their keel becomes buried. Miles from nowhere, the vessel is trapped, and if there isn't another boat in the area to assist them or a tug is not available to pull them off, the boat is lost.

A novice sailor can easily be spotted at Long Point, not by his new shiny plastic boat, but because he can be seen sitting high and dry on Bluff Bar with the outdrive buried in the sand. His first question to his rescuer is usually, "Where is Bluff Bar?"

The condition of wooden sail and steam vessels was also a contributing factor to losses. Some were not in sufficient repair to stand the punishment of the violent late-fall storms off Long Point.

The early builders of ships sailing the Great Lakes were skilled craftsmen. These ships were constructed by hand up until the late 1880s, built of the finest white oak, planked and framed. Even with the best expertise in shipbuilding and the finest materials, the lifespan of a wooden ship was about 15 years. After this time they started to deteriorate. As decay set in, it was an endless job keeping them in seaworthy condition. Each additional year meant some major repair work.

Some owners or captains would be a bit stingy about spending the money to keep their vessel in shipshape. They could sometimes get away with this, until they were caught in one of Long Point's notorious November snow squalls or storms. The vessel's decaying hull, pounded by the raging sea, would start taking on water faster than the pumps could handle it and would eventually slip beneath the waves. This cause of ship loss was not unique to Long Point, but also occurred in other areas on the Great Lakes where destructive storms were common. A vessel might also have trouble at sea if the crew were too few or too inexperienced to manage the vessel properly in bad weather.

Extending along the entire length of the south side of Long Point are a series of sandbars. Some of these are located close to shore, others some distance off. These shifting sandbars have been responsible for the loss of many lives and vessels. There were also a number of vessels that became stranded on the bars, and some of these had the good fortune of being able to get off. Some were able to have the cargo and ship salvaged, others a complete loss.

In bad weather a ship could damage its rudder or have its sails blown out, thereby losing complete control. Dragging an anchor to stop going up on the bar was often times fruitless, with the end result of the ship becoming grounded on the bar. Sometimes the crew made it safely to shore, other times the waters were so turbulent they drowned in the pounding surf.

Not all the vessels wrecked off Long Point met their demise due to these reasons. Some were wrecked because of the unscrupulous actions of the "blackbirds."

Blackbirding was a maritime practice all over the world. A blackbirder would set up a false light some distance from the lighthouse. There he would lure the vessel to shore and eventually trap a victim.

A ship sailing down the Point in bad weather or a fog would see this light. The captain, thinking he was at the end of the Point, would alter his course and attempt to round the tip. To the dismay of the crew, the vessel would become grounded on a shoal. The blackbirders would wait, making no attempt to rescue the terrorized crew, who would be lost while trying to reach shore. Those who made it would stagger down the beach seeking help, getting no aid from the looters.

Not only did they catch those who were attracted by the false light, but other ships that were driven ashore by storms. The blackbirds would plunder the cargo of the distressed vessel and rob the bodies of the perished sailors.

It was reported that an instance of such piracy occurred when the schooner *Greenbush* was driven ashore in a December during the late 1800s. She was swept onto a shoal and the entire crew was lost while trying to get ashore. As soon as the storm died down the blackbirds removed the cargo of flour and sold it on the mainland.

Long Point was an ideal place for these wreckers to carry on their foul deeds. Being so isolated and accessible only by water, here they could carry on their trade without concern about the authorities. Once people on the mainland began to suspect this gang of murderous thieves, they refused to purchase their contraband. Eventually the blackbirds had to flee from this area for fear of being caught.

Another reason ships were lost off the Point was because of that extra last trip. Owners and captains of vessels would try to get an extra trip in before freeze-up. This meant money in their pockets but also, on a number of occasions, it meant the loss of a ship, crew and cargo.

During the late fall and early winter, the terrible southwest gales of Long Point wreaked havoc and destruction on those who sailed Lake Erie's waters.

Crews caught in these storms would sometimes frantically throw what cargo they could over the side to lighten their ship, hoping this action would save them from a watery grave. Often this exercise didn't help their plight, and the icy cold water claimed its victims.

Those who benefitted from this last trip were the people who lived along the mainland near Long Point. One man's loss was another's gain as the cargoes from the lost ships washed ashore — lumber, wool, hardware, coal and practically anything else a poor struggling settler could use. It is reported by some of the old-timers that a number of barns built in the Port Rowan and St. Williams area were constructed out of timbers taken from wrecked ships.

One of the last major causes of wrecks on the south shore of Long Point was the existence of the Cut, which joined the lake and the bay. The location of this channel was west of the entrance of the new provincial park, near the now land-locked lighthouse. This lighthouse was built during 1879 to assist mariners in locating the opening.

As early as 1828 a petition to the provincial government was drafted expressing the need for a channel through the isthmus. Why was the need for a channel so strongly requested? During the War of 1812 the British had experienced great difficulty when moving their troops, supplies and cannon to the western end of Lake Erie. The biggest obstacle along their route was Long Point.

When they came to Long Point, they either had to go around the end of the tip, which could be disastrous during bad weather, or drag all their supplies and boats across land near the carrying place. This was the narrowest piece of land on the Point, joining the lake and the bay.

They had heavy boats used by the settlers to transport corn and flour, batteaux and small boats to portage. Rowing these heavy batteaux 30 miles a day, then carrying these and all their supplies across this neck of land was very strenuous and time-consuming work. Haste was essential when planning to trap and encounter the enemy.

When the war was over, the British authorities realized they had to be better prepared if hostilities with the United States broke out again. To move troops and supplies with expedience and less effort, a channel was required at Long Point. Also, as civilization developed along the shoreline of the Great Lakes and water traffic increased, a western channel became essential.

This channel was to play an important part by giving many ships safe passage through the opening, those that didn't want to take the long and dangerous journey around the end and others that sought shelter from violent storms on the lake.

However 31 wrecks occurred in the near vicinity of the entrance to the Cut. Along with these were a number of vessels that were stranded on the shoals but were fortunate enough to be able to get off.

At times the prevailing southwest winds blowing at gale force made it difficult to hit the entrance to the Cut. A ship under sail had only one chance to make it to safety. Missing the channel opening, the vessel had no turning room and ended up either beached or washed aground on a bar. Eventually the victim would be broken to pieces by the pounding surf.

During 1833 a survey was made by N.H. Baird, a civil engineer, and Captain John Harris, R.N. Their recommendations of where and how the Cut should be built was expected by the Legislative Assembly. However, by a fluke of nature during November 1833, a storm with high-velocity winds pushed the water right through the Point, carving a channel from the lake to the inner bay. This channel was approximately 380 yards wide and the depth ranged from 11 feet to 18 feet. Piers were built to ensure the channel would stay open. In 1840 a lightship was positioned in the inner bay to assist in marking the opening.

The Cut gradually eroded and partly filled in. In 1865 another storm carved a new Cut just west of the first one. By storm action over the years, it became over 20 feet deep and half a mile wide.

During 1879 the wooden lighthouse (which is still standing) was built. This light continued to operate until 1916, even though the Cut ceased to exist after 1906. That year brought a storm that completely filled it in.

Some strange things happened to some of the vessels seeking the entrance to the Cut during bad storms. One was during 1865, when the schooner *Louisa*, sailing out of Wallaceburg with a cargo of scrap iron, had her sails blow out near the channel. Being at the mercy of the waves and wind, she was fortunate to be carried right through the cut and into the bay. The undamaged vessel remained there all that winter.

Two schooners, the *Rebecca Foster* in 1861 and the *Sam Amsden* in 1862, both caught in violent storms, were carried overland without benefit of water from the south shore to the bay. The *Rebecca Foster* was a complete loss, while the hull of the *Sam Amsden* was salvaged.

The Old Cut lighthouse still stands as a reminder of the part it played in guiding ships safely to their destinations, and it's also a reminder of those who met their doom in the waters on the south side.

Other causes that contributed to ships being lost include overloading of a vessel with too much cargo, bad stowage of cargo, too much deck cargo, fire, absence of navigational aids until 1830, and finally, one which sums it all up, "bad judgement."

During July 1981 old human bones from the remains of three skeletons were found on Long Point. The next year five skulls were discovered. Both these findings were reported to the Ontario Provincial Police. After the investigation these were sent to the forensic centre in Toronto. The dating of these remains was estimated at 500 to 1000 A.D.

The Earliest Shipwrecks with Loss of Life off Long Point

One would think that the first marine casualties off Long Point would be the vessels of the French explorers in the seventeenth century. If not them, then the vessels transporting merchandise and settlers to develop a new nation out of this wilderness in the eighteenth and nineteenth centuries. Or perhaps some of these earliest losses were ships built by the British to protect this young nation.

None of these qualify as the first losses off Long Point shores. This distinction belongs to those who inhabited this part of the world long before the white man came. Aboriginal watercraft were the first to suc-

cumb to Long Point's treacherous waters.

The Indians travelled the upper and lower lakes and rivers, trading, making war and seeking new fishing and hunting grounds. Paddling their canoes along the shoreline or launching them at the portage could at times spell disaster. These canoes could have one or many on board, depending on their mission. They could be loaded with cargo such as game, fish, furs, implements of war, tools, goods required to set up a base camp, or other necessities. During a storm, their small craft could be upset before they could reach shore, dumping them and their contents into the

The writer getting some knowledge from two archaeologists, Jamie Fox and Ann Brydon, during an archaeological survey done on Long Point in 1984. — Dave Stone

foaming surf, the upset canoes dashed to pieces on a bar or the beach, the occupants left to drown.

The strength, quality and manoeuvrability of a canoe depended on construction materials available in the area. Some had to resort to building their vessels out of hollow logs, which were clumsy and unmanageable. Others built elegant birchbark canoes that were swift and had the seaworthiness of some of the finest built today.

Artifacts have been found from tribes as early as 340 B.C. and as late as 1450 A.D. at a site close to the tip of the Point. In the summer of 1984, some 5,000-year-old artifacts were found in the Bluff Pond area.

There are no records to date showing that Long Point was used as a permanent base, such as the establishment of a village. It really wasn't necessary to live out there year-round. There were plenty of fish and game on the mainland. Besides, living on Long Point was too dangerous. A warring tribe could attack an unsuspecting victim from both sides with no escape route. But whitefish abounded off Long Point shores and this brought Indians to the area. Families would move out to Long Point in the fall of the year to catch and smoke their winter needs. Once they had their requirements, they would return to their permanent villages. Many travelled great distances to this favourite fishing grounds.

During 1981 and 1982 human skulls and skeletons were found on Long Point. These are now thought to be those of the Algonquin, dating from 500 to 1000 A.D.

Up until 1650 the first growers of tobacco populated this section of Ontario. They were named Neutrals by the French explorers because they traded with both the Huron Indians and their enemies, the Iroquois. The tribe's Indian name was Attawandron.

They were eventually driven out by the Iroquois, a great number were slaughtered and their lands taken over for hunting and fishing. The survivors were forced into northern Ontario and eventually merged with other tribes to form the Wyandots.

During March 1818 the Wyandot Indians, who were living on the north shore of Lake Ontario, engaged in a naval battle off Long Point with the Senecas, who were living on the south shore of Lake Ontario. The war between the two tribes started because the wife of a Seneca chief was carried off by a Wyandot prince. War started immediately with great slaughter and cruelty. At the final battle the Wyandots were beaten and had to flee for their lives. They were followed to Lake Huron by the Senecas. When the Wyandots reached the straits, they found them frozen and had to leap from ice floe to ice floe. The Senecas stopped chasing them, since they didn't want to take a chance on the ice.

The Wyandots now found themselves with the Ottawas, Pottawatomies and Chippewas, who greeted them as friends and made them welcome. They were fitted out with a large fleet of birchbark canoes and set off to pursue the enemy.

Prehistoric artifacts found by Dave Stone on Long Point. These were donated to the Ontario Ministry of Citizenship and Culture.
— Dave Stone

The Wyandots went along the north shore of Lake Erie, as far as Long Point, and here they stopped, sending a party to investigate the strength of the Senecas. They encountered their equal number in a Seneca scouting party, and both parties returned to their fleets.

The Wyandots took their birchbark canoes to the end of the Point, and then, with the enemy in sight, headed out into the lake. The Senecas followed them in their clumsy log canoes.

Suddenly, in their swift birchbark canoes, they turned and attacked the Senecas. It was no contest, the Seneca canoes were sunk and the men were slaughtered off Long Point by the Wyandots. This was a major disaster for the Senecas. They were all slain, except one brave, who was allowed to live so he could tell his tribe of their defeat.

This ended the war between these two tribes, but left Long Point bloodstained.

No one will ever know the number of lives lost over the centuries by the native peoples in the area of the Point.

In September 1984 I had the pleasure of spending several days with William Fox, regional archaeologist, and his crew, who were doing an archaeological survey on Long Point.

Unfortunately a great amount of pre-historic information has been lost due to high water. A great number of the sites have been destroyed.

The only way that one can get information about life on Long Point is by the finding of artifacts. Pottery, arrowheads, tools, animal and fish bones, all tell a story of the native past. Fox and his crew located artifacts which escaped my notice. When one is looking for a piece of history, one has to know what one is looking for.

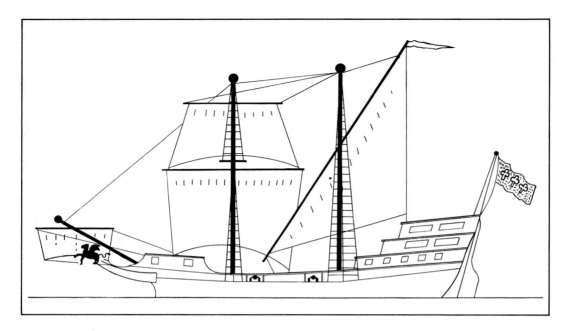

*LaSalle's barque
the Griffon, 1679.*

The First Ship to Sail Around Long Point

In 1679 LaSalle, the famed French explorer, built the *Griffon* near the mouth of Cayuga Creek, in the county of Niagara, where the village of LaSalle is now located.

LaSalle wanted to build a substantial ship to explore the upper lakes. Like most of the early explorers, he was in poor financial shape. Using the *Griffon* in the fur trade could relieve this situation. Thus far his exploits had only been partially subsidized by the king. He tried to make ends meet by his wits, barterings and promises.

The actual building of the *Griffon* was supervised by two of his companions, Father Louis Hennepin, a Recollect priest, and Henry De Tonty. LaSalle was absent during most of the construction, as he was at Fort Frontenac looking after his own troubled affairs.

Prior to the actual construction, LaSalle had sent an advance party to Green Bay on Lake Michigan. These men were to trade with the Indians and obtain a large quantity of furs. When the *Griffon* was launched, she was to sail to this destination with the tradesmen and materials to build another ship. This ship would be used to explore the Mississippi . Once LaSalle reached the advance party, plans were to load the furs on board and transport them to a storehouse he had built above Niagara Falls, then ship them back to Fort Frontenac to help pay off his creditors.

Construction of the vessel was difficult in this vast wilderness, and from time to time the builders were harassed by members of the Seneca tribe, who disapproved of the building of this ship. Several times the

Senecas had planned to burn her but were not successful, thanks mainly to an Indian woman who would inform the French of the Indians' plans.

LaSalle's group of 16 men, along with Moise Hillaret, a master shipwright, and Tonty, kept hard at work building the barque all that winter, and the vessel was ready for launch in May 1679. Another arson threat by the Seneca caused the ship to be launched sooner than expected.

She slid off the stocks and into the river with a small ceremony and was named the *Griffon* in honour of Count Frontenac, whose coat of arms bore the figure of this mythical animal. Three guns were fired, Father Hennepin said a *Te Deum*, and brandy was offered to all those in attendance, including the Indians.

Three months later the *Griffon* was completely outfitted with provisions, arms, merchandise and seven cannon. On August 7, 1679, she was on her way with a party of 32 on board. The barque caught the fresh breezes and sailed beautifully into Lake Erie.

Without charts to warn the crew of impending danger, the *Griffon* sailed on. LaSalle was aware of the dangers of Long Point because he had seen a rough chart made by Galinée in 1669. However, he had no idea where Long Point was, since he was sailing in a thick fog.

He heard the sound of breakers and realized danger was near. He altered course, but still heard the sounds of the waves breaking on the shore. LaSalle sounded continuously but could not locate the bottom.

Suddenly the fog started to lift and a sailor reported that the soundings had decreased to three fathoms. Awaiting the lifting of the brume, the famed voyager found the low sand cape of Long Point stretched out before him.

LaSalle's caution and vigilance had saved him from becoming the first ship wreck on Long Point. Instead the *Griffon* became the first ship to sail around Long Point, the first in Lake Erie, and the first on Lake Huron and Lake Michigan. LaSalle was so grateful to be spared disaster on Long Point's treacherous shoals that he named this sandspit "Cape St. Francis."

The *Griffon* then proceeded from Erie, up the St. Clair River, and eventually into Lake Huron, then Lake Michigan and on to Green Bay. Here he met some of the party he had sent out over a year ago. He found shelter in a small bay, now Detroit harbour, and loaded on board 12,000 pounds of beaver and buffalo pelts. He picked a crew of six to take the ship back to Niagara. The *Griffon* sailed on September 18, 1679.

The directions given to Luc, the pilot, were to stop at Mickilimackinac, drop some supplies off for LaSalle, then proceed to Niagara. With a shot from her cannon the four-month-old *Griffon* disappeared with her crew, never to be seen again.

A year later LaSalle met a party of Pottawattomie Indians near Lake Simcoe. They told him they had seen the *Griffon* two days after she left Green Bay. She was at anchor in a sheltered bay off northern Lake Michigan. A raging storm had come up and the Indians had urged Luc to stay there till it was over. Luc had laughed at them and told the small band that the *Griffon* was a sturdy ship and could take any kind of storm. The Indians claimed that the last time they saw the *Griffon*, it was having difficulty in the violent waters and was being driven out to the Huron Islands.

LaSalle heard a conflicting rumour later. He was told that their supposed "friends," the Pottawattomie Indians, had captured the ship and burned her. LaSalle also suspected that the pilot, Luc, who had previously proved himself untrustworthy, had made off with the furs and had headed for the French River, where LaSalle's enemies were plying the fur trade.

LaSalle was heartbroken over the loss of his ship, but he did manage to carry on his explorations of both the Mississippi and Missouri rivers. His life came to an end at the age of 43, when he was murdered by his own men in Texas on March 19, 1687.

Years have passed into centuries since the *Griffon*'s disappearance. Around the Great Lakes there have

Orrie Vail and Dave Stone having a discussion about the Griffon. — Dave Stone

been numerous claims of it having been found at various locations. These claims have all been disputed, with the exception of one that for a lengthy time some researchers felt certain was LaSalle's ship. This claim was made by Orrie Vail of Tobermory.

Vail found the ship's remains in four or five feet of water in a cove off Russel Island, two miles northwest of Tobermory, Ontario.

For 50 years Vail kept his secret to himself, until he confided in 1955 to John MacLean, a reporter from the Toronto *Telegram*. MacLean some years later wrote the book *The Fate of The Griffon* with the assistance of C.H.J. Snider, a world-recognized authority on early Canadian ships, who made a thorough investigation of the remains and noted it as a most important Canadian discovery. With Snider was Canada's outstanding marine artist Rowley W. Murphy, who spent 25 years researching the *Griffon*. Murphy said the wreck matched in every detail the drawings made by Father Louis Hennepin, LaSalle's priest, who had sketched the ship as it was being built. The thoughts of Murphy and Snider as to the verification of the wreck were published in the historical journals.

Many years after the work of Orrie Vail, John MacLean, C.J.S. Snider and Rowley Murphy had been completed, there were those who were still skeptical about the identity of the ship. With all four men deceased, a thorough study was made of the remains in the 1980s. Results of the study show that the wreckage found on Russel Island was that of a ship constructed between 1840-1860 not in 1679.

These published results were not only a severe blow to Tobermory, but to all of Canada; it was the loss of an important artifact in our nation's history. With none of the original researchers alive today, there is no one left to defend these aging timbers.

Where are the remains of the 45-ton barque today?

As it sailed around Long Point and escaped being wrecked at the tip, little did Rene Cavelier Sieur De La Salle realize he would soon lose the *Griffon* in a cloud of mystery.

The memory of the *Griffon* has outlived all other ships that have sailed on the Great Lakes to date.

Crew members of H.M.S. Mohawk burying the payroll on a sandy ridge on Long Point.
— Artist: K.W. Hawkins

H.M.S. Mohawk and Buried Treasure on Long Point

Fact or fiction, the story is told of the loss of the British sloop H.M.S. *Mohawk*, in use on Lake Erie during the War of 1812.

The *Mohawk* was in Port Dover when the American forces were approaching that port. The Americans, under command of Colonel Campbell, planned to invade the Long Point area, burn the mills and seize the British forces' supplies. Campbell sailed with five vessels and 800 troops.

On board *Mohawk* was the payroll for the militia, all in coin and long overdue. It was to be distributed to the poor soldiers along the shoreline.

Fearing capture, the *Mohawk* sailed out of Port Dover before the invading forces arrived. The sloop proceeded to an area on Long Point. A party went ashore and buried the payroll. If the ship were captured, this payroll would not fall into the invaders' hands.

But the sloop, supposedly sailing from Courtwright Ridge and battling heavy seas near the Bluff Bar area, was swamped by a violent storm. Only two members of the crew survived the sinking. Campbell and his invading forces encountered the same storm, which delayed them from reaching Canadian soil for two

Ben Harris, a great friend and keeper for the Long Point Company for many years, with his dog Curly. — Mrs. Ben Harris

days. They eventually reached Port Dover and did burn the village and the mills to the ground.

Stories are told about treasure hunters who have tried to find the missing cache, but the location of the payroll still remains one of Long Point's secrets. Is it buried on a sandy beach, on one of the wind-swept dunes, in a marshy bog, or under a large oak tree. Standing guard over this secret are Long Point's sentinels, the wildlife who make this land their habitat.

Early records of vessels employed by the British Naval Service on the Great Lakes are incomplete, which makes it very difficult to substantiate this event. There was a sloop called the *Mohawk* built in 1795 and used by the British for a period of time. The date of its loss, however, appears to be 1803 not 1814. But earlier accounts of Great Lakes military shipping are very difficult to assess, as records were lost or were not exact.

The military frequently commandeered private vessels for use, and quite often no records were made of such transactions or regarding the period of time a ship was in military service.

My favourite treasure hunt story is one recounted by Ben Harris, my best Long Point friend and keeper for the Long Point Company.

After the last war, two men from the nearby area came by boat to the part of Long Point where Ben Harris was keeping. With them they brought supplies, enough to last them for a week, including a suitcase full of whisky and, most important, a metal detector. (Metal detectors had developed considerably during wartime and were now available from suppliers.) These two men were quite certain that the *Mohawk* payroll was buried in this vicinity and sought Ben's assistance in locating the treasure.

The keeper's shanty on Long Point where the treasure hunters pulled up the floorboards looking for the cache. — Mrs. Ben Harris

For two days they used their detector with no success. They had been eaten by every type of insect, fallen in bogs, scared by the wampers and loaded with wood ticks. In the evening they would sit in Ben's cabin, drinking a fair quantity of whisky, and the stories would develop as to what they were going to do with all the money once it had been located.

On the third night, Ben asked them for a demonstration of the detector. They brought it into the cabin and began sweeping it back and forth across the floor. Immediately the alarm went off, and they were certain they had a good find.

Trying it again they found that in one place on the floor the alarm was very strong. Their search was over. The treasure was right under the floorboards of Ben's cabin. Immediately they started to tear up the floorboards, much to Ben's dismay.

Alas, the so-called treasure was not a chest of silver coins but the metal casing for the old hand pump that looked after supplying water for the cabin.

To overcome their disappointment the treasure hunters got very drunk. When morning came they were disgusted with their lot and also very hung over. Realizing their folly, they packed their gear and left Ben Harris and Long Point forever.

Ben had found them entertaining for a few days but was now glad to see them leave. Looking around the cabin after their departure, he discovered that they hadn't left him so much as a heel in a bottle. What they had left was a large hole in the cabin floor, which kept Ben occupied for the entire day.

A group of Irish immigrants spent their first few days in Canada living in the dunes of Long Point and waiting for rescue. — Dave Stone

Wreck Number One: Young Phoenix

On an early fall day in September 1818 a large group of Irish immigrants boarded the schooner *Young Phoenix*. This was to be the last leg of their journey and, they thought, the easiest. They had just crossed the Atlantic Ocean, coming from Tipperary, Ireland. Accommodations for immigrants on ocean crossings were not the best. They had been subjected to cramped quarters, a poor diet and unsanitary conditions. They boarded the ship at Buffalo, New York, paying $50 a head for passage to Port Talbot, Ontario. Here they were going to start a new life, with all its hopes and promises.

The weather, while not the best, was fairly typical of mid-September and did not appear to pose any added hazard. But as the trip across Lake Erie progressed, conditions worsened. Passing Long Point *Young Phoenix* started taking on water. The captain, hoping he could save the ship, tried to run her to the beach. He soon realized that they would not make it, so he gave the order to abandon ship. The boats were put out and the vessel was cleared of all passengers and crew. They all made it safely to shore.

On board they had left their only earthly possessions. *Young Phoenix* sank in 110 feet of water, two and a half miles southwest of the tip of Long Point. The immigrants' possessions sank to the bottom along with $5,000 in the captain's strong box.

The passengers and crew were stranded on the end of Long Point. There was no lighthouse keeper on the Point to offer them assistance, for the first lighthouse was not built until 1830. They spent the next few days among the sand dunes, frantically waving at every passing ship. Finally a schooner saw their plight, took them all on board and on to their destination.

These early settlers would never forget their first time ashore in Canada. They were very fortunate. Many of the wrecks that followed took a great number of lives.

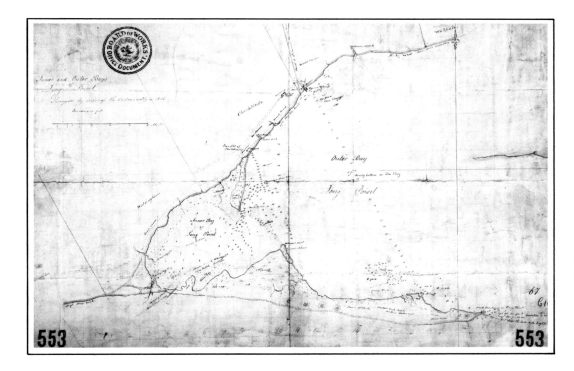

553 553

The Portage or Carrying Place, Long Point, 1816. Inner and outer bays of Long Point. Surveyed by order of the Admiralty, 1816. — Canadian Hydrographic Service, Environment Canada

The Proposed Naval Arsenal for Long Point and the Role of the Carrying Place

During 1793 Lieutenant-Governor John Graves Simcoe was convinced that Long Point and its surrounding waters would make an excellent site for a naval arsenal. His proposal was turned down by Lord Dorchester, the Governor General, who thought the area would be unhealthy for the troops living there. He also turned down Simcoe's recommendations for a blockhouse and a garrison for the same reason. So the Point never did get a military or naval establishment.

However Long Point did play an important role as a portage for British soldiers during the War of 1812. The sandy peninsula thrusting out into Lake Erie was used as a stopover for 40 British regular soldiers, 200 militia and Indian guides on their way to defend Amherstburg against the American aggressors.

General Brock, Lieutenant-Governor for Upper Canada, left York on August 6, 1812. He went to Port Dover, assembling his troops on the way, then left Port Dover for Amherstburg with his troops.

One of Brock's officers, Major Salmon, sailed on the small schooner *Chippewa*, accompanied by a number of bateaux and small boats. He left Port Dover on August 8, 1812, with a detachment of soldiers. The trip was slow because many of the small boats were in poor condition. These boats leaked badly, and every

Long Point Portage — Lettering on the plaque reads as follows: This portage, which crossed the isthmus joining Long Point to the mainland, was used by travellers in small craft following the north shore of Lake Erie in order to avoid the open waters and length of journey around the Point. Although used earlier by the Indians, the portage was first recorded in 1670 by two Sulpician missionaries, Francis de Casson and Rene de Brehaut de Galinee. For about one hundred and fifty years traffic increased over the carrying place, first as a result of the French expansion to the southwest, including the founding of Detroit in 1701, and after 1783, because of the movement of settlers into this region. The portage was abandoned in 1833 when a storm broke a navigable channel through the isthmus.
— Dave Stone

so often they would have to go ashore and bail out. No chances could be taken with wet cargoes, as they were carrying smoothbores, flints, flintlocks and cartridges. Eventually they made it to the portage.

Another group that sailed from Port Dover had great difficulty finding the Carrying Place. Unable to locate the small creek that would lead them to the portage, the party anchored in among the rushes and settled down for the night. The next day they sighted General Brock and his party in their boats. They proceeded to the Carrying Place but had great difficulty portaging one of their boats. The weight of the six-pounder gun on board was just about all they could manage.

General Brock and his flotilla portaged overland at the Carrying Place and proceeded to Port Talbot. Here they camped overnight. Brock's fleet was led by an open boat which contained the general and his aides. The lead boat carried a flaming torch at night.

With the heavy batteaux they could only travel approximately 48 kilometres a day. It took five days to complete their strenuous 240-kilometre journey.

After winning the admiration and help of Tecumseh at Amherstburg, Brock received the unexpected surrender of General Hull, leader of the American forces at Detroit.

Throughout the War of 1812, Long Point and this portage played an important role in the transportation system of Upper Canada, especially after the Niagara region was occupied by the Americans.

With the development of the Lake Erie region after the War of 1812, waterborne traffic grew tremendously, and the need for a channel to join the lake and the bay was evident. In September 1828 a petition to the provincial government was drafted expressing the need for a channel traversing the isthmus. Richard Baird, an English civil engineer, and Captain John Harris, R.N., were commissioned to do a survey. When it was finished, Sir John Colborne, Lieutenant-Governor, studied their proposal.

The north side of the Portage or Carrying Place.
— Dave Stone

Before authorization was given to begin this endeavour, nature stepped in and rendered a storm that cut a channel 390 yards wide and 12-18 feet deep. Once the channel opened, the portage passed into history. The traveller could now cross from the lake to the bay with ease and safety.

There is an historical plaque, erected and dedicated in 1973, marking the site of the Carrying Place that our forefathers used. The only activity here now is that of the tourists who come to read about their heritage. But much more can be observed if one comes here in the quiet of the early morning. Faintly heard are the shouts of men hauling heavy bateaux overland, and here and there appear brilliant flashes of red from British officers' tunics. Over on the bay side, the sound of paddles interrupts the tranquility of the morning as the adventurers' canoes approach the Carrying Place.

Rialto

Seth W. Johnson and A. Whipple of Cleveland, Ohio, were the original owners of this 84-foot two-masted scow. *Rialto* was built in Cleveland in 1846 by Johnson and Tisdale. The scow had a short life span of only five years. However, during its five years, it had some interesting experiences.

In 1848 her new captain and owner, Captain Gale, had the *Rialto* anchored near the Old Cut. Captain Gale was suspected of smuggling or stealing anchors, or both of these offenses. The customs officer and several men went out to arrest the captain. When they reached the vessel, it was riding at anchor in the bay with her mainsail set. Captain Gale welcomed the men aboard and asked them below to have a drink, which they proceeded to do. With the cabin door closed they didn't know that the anchor had been raised and the vessel was sailing. When the customs officer and his men finally came up on deck, the *Rialto* was out on the lake and heading for a United States port. The captain treated his guests with respect, making sure their wants were looked after, while the *Rialto* made her way to Buffalo. After a short stay, she headed back to the Canadian side, and the kidnapped party eventually ended up back at Port Rowan. Their remarks upon arrival were not recorded — but Captain Gale sailed on to other episodes.

Over the next few years the *Rialto* kept busy moving freight around the lake. Then, while sailing off Long Point on July 1, 1851, under the command of a Captain Gaffett, the *Rialto* was hit by a sudden gust of wind and overturned. She went bottom up and stayed that way for most of the afternoon. Her destination had been the Sand Hills, west of Long Point, for a load of lumber. On this trip down the lake she carried no ballast. The crew, with the exception of the first mate, pulled themselves up on the overturned hull. The first mate was washed away from the outstretched hands of the sailors trying to save him. The heavy seas carried him out further into the lake and he disappeared from view. The captain was particularly grief stricken upon learning that his wife had been trapped inside the cabin when the ship capsized.

The survivors clung to the overturned vessel for five hours. They were finally sighted by the schooner *Carrington*, which was en route to Tonawanda. The *Rialto*'s crew was taken off, and as they were leaving, another strong gust of wind prevailed. This righted the *Rialto* and there stood Mrs. Gaffett, safe and sound. She had been trapped in an air pocket in the hull and managed to stay alive. Two lives were saved, as Mrs. Gaffett was expecting a baby in two months. The *Rialto* was a total loss, but the survivors were returned safely to port.

Old-timers think this could be the remains of the Henry Clay *but this has yet to be proven. — Dave Stone*

Henry Clay

In 1826 the *Henry Clay*, a wooden steamer, started her career running between Buffalo and Detroit. She would sail every fourth day from either port. She had a 60-horsepower engine and was classed as an elegant steamship. Her cabins were comfortable and expensively fitted to suit the wealthy traveller of that time. She was named after the famed United States orator and statesman Henry Clay. She was a profitable vessel during her lifetime, and around the lakes she had a reputation of being a good ship. In 1827 she became the first steamer to reach Sault Ste. Marie.

On October 24, 1851, she sailed from Buffalo bound for Detroit with a cargo of flour and baled wool. On the night of October 25 she ran into a gale off Long Point. Due to the high waves that were severely beating her hull, her cargo shifted onto her engine. This made the vessel impossible to handle. She got into a trough, and then a mountainous wave tore the deck from the hull, taking ten of the crew with it. At this point the *Henry Clay* rolled over, drowning the rest of the crew with the exception of one. This lone survivor came ashore on an overturned yawl. He was later picked up by a passing schooner.

The *Henry Clay*'s cargo of baled wool was scattered along the beaches of Long Point and kept the spinning wheels in Port Rowan going for years. Her hull was washed ashore and was buried in the sand at the tip of Long Point for many years. There it stayed until recent high lake levels uncovered it and washed it from its resting place and back out into the lake.

The *Henry Clay* was the major disaster on the Great Lakes in 1851. Captain George Collard and 15 members of his crew were lost the night the *Henry Clay* went down.

The loss of the steamer Atlantic was Long Point's most serious marine disaster. This elegant ship went down with 300 lives in 1852.

The Atlantic — One of the Major Marine Disasters in the History of the Great Lakes

The story of the sinking of the *Atlantic* has more to it than the loss of lives and a ship in Lake Erie. It also includes the search by divers for the treasure that went down with her and the attempt to examine the sunken *Atlantic* with the first submarine on the Great Lakes.

On Thursday evening, August 19, 1852, the sidewheel steamer *Atlantic* left the port of Buffalo bound for Monroe, Michigan. She was a beautiful ship and elegantly fitted out. Not only did the *Atlantic* have good looks, but she was fast. During her first year, 1849, she had set a record from Buffalo to Detroit of 16½ hours. The steamer was built in 1849 by John L. Wolverton at Marine City, Michigan, for E.B. Ward of Detroit, and was operated by the Michigan Central Railroad Company. The *Atlantic* was 265 feet long and had a gross tonnage of 1,155 tons.

She was three years old on the evening she sailed. In command was Captain C.B. Turner from Oswego, a lake captain with 18 years experience, on board were approximately 550 to 600 people. (It is difficult to assess exactly how many were on board, as the trip sheet was lost.) A great number of the passengers were Norwegian immigrants heading for the West to establish new homes. This was to be the beginning of a new life for these settlers. They carried with them on the ship all their worldly possessions. Little did they realize at the time of sailing that more than half of them would never make it to the fertile land they were seeking.

Around 2 a.m. all aboard were sleeping except those on watch. Off Long Point the waters were dead calm. Visibility was hazy, but the stars could be seen. As the *Atlantic* proceeded on her course the 275-foot *Ogdensburg* approached, without Captain Turner's knowledge. This propeller steamer was owned by the Northern Transportation Company. She had come from Cleveland and was bound for Grand Bay. Her course had been changed to hard port to make the Welland Canal.

The bow of the *Ogdensburg* rammed the unsuspecting *Atlantic* just forward of the port wheelbox, leaving a large hole below the waterline. Just before the collision, the *Ogdensburg* reversed engines, and it was thought at the time that no serious damage had been done. Both vessels continued on their courses in the darkness.

The *Atlantic* kept going without missing a stroke of her walking beam, until water put her fires out. As the ship started to list, the crew moved passengers and freight to the other side, but this did not help. The *Atlantic*'s master headed the vessel to shore, not realizing at the time that he was making a grave error which would cost many lives. He had hoped to run her into shallow water or run her aground before she sank.

With the fires now out and the *Ogdensburg* two miles away, no help was available and the *Atlantic* began sinking by the bow. Panic spread like wildfire. Two boats were lowered, but too many passengers tried to get into these boats. They were upset and many were drowned. Before the fires went out, while the *Atlantic* was still underway, many leaped overboard only to be crushed in the paddlewheels. The alarm had been given to abandon ship, but in many cases orders were not followed, as the Norwegians couldn't understand English. Wooden deck chairs, gear, doors, furniture, anything that would float was thrown over the side. People clung to the debris in the darkness. There was now no command on board, as Captain Turner had been seriously injured while assisting to lower a lifeboat.

The *Ogdensburg*, several miles away, could hear the screams of terror and rushed to the scene, where it picked up 250 survivors from the water. This was a very difficult task, as they did their searching in the darkness. A number of passengers and crew clung to the stern, which was buoyed by air in the after hold, and were rescued. The stern stayed afloat after the bow had hit bottom. Once all the trapped air escaped, it went to the bottom in 160 feet of water off the tip of Long Point.

The survivors were transported by the *Ogdensburg* to Erie, Pennsylvania. Fate sometimes smiles on the unfortunate, and such was the case for the 60 Norwegians who had been refused passage on the *Atlantic* for not having the necessary tickets and funds.

An 1852 Detroit newspaper stated the following: "The late *Atlantic* — We notice that the United States marshal has published a notice to the owner of the propellor *Ogdensburg* to appear in court at Steubenville, Ohio, to show cause why she should not be sold under a libel filed in said court by the Messrs. Ward, charging her with running into and sinking the *Atlantic*, causing them the loss of one hundred thousand dollars."

Today the *Atlantic* lies at the bottom, in the middle of the shipping lanes, off Long Point. Since 1852 many ships have passed over her watery grave and the tomb of those unfortunate souls, not realizing the terror that prevailed on Friday, August 20, 1852.

This *Atlantic* was not the first or the last vessel by that name to be shipwrecked. From 1846 to 1963 nine ships named *Atlantic* were lost in the Great Lakes and other U.S. waters.

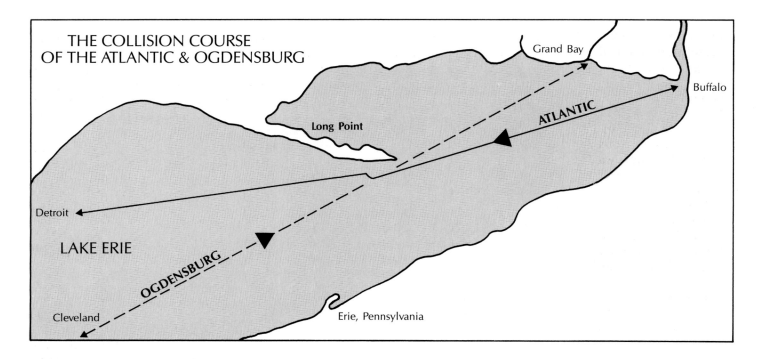

THE COLLISION COURSE
OF THE ATLANTIC & OGDENSBURG

Grand Bay

Buffalo

ATLANTIC

Long Point

Detroit

LAKE ERIE

OGDENSBURG

Cleveland

Erie, Pennsylvania

Salvage Attempts on the Atlantic

J.B. Green, Elliott P. Harrington, Lodner Philips, Harry Gamble, Roland B. Smith, Jack C. Holzer, Jack Maythem and Gary Kozak have all found the location of the *Atlantic* and some have attempted to carry out some sort of salvage operation.

Diving for the *Atlantic* today has its problems, one of them being that she lies beneath the shipping lanes. A large amount of big ship traffic heading to and from the Welland Canal or going into Nanticoke pass over her. It's like trying to dig a hole in the middle of a superhighway during a holiday weekend.

The American Express Company, one of the big losers when the *Atlantic* went down, hired J.B. Green in 1853 to locate their strong box, which contained a sum totalling $35,000. Green was a well-known salvage diver and had done many dives around the lake. From his previous diving operations, he had had a diver's suit made out of India rubber and copper. However he had never attempted a dive as deep as the *Atlantic*, so he used the special equipment supplied by the New York firm that hired him.

He made his first attempt in 1853, but this dive was aborted when the pumps failed. On this dive he had reached a depth of 110 feet. On the next dive he became stuck in the smokestack, began losing air and had to be pulled up. On the third attempt he reached the deck but again had air hose problems and had to come up. When he had to return to Buffalo to make repairs, the search was discontinued.

Green later returned to the site of the sinking,

located the wreck and once again dove on her. The vessel had changed position and the bow was now lying southeast. The last time he saw the ship it had been lying southwest. During this dive he located the cabin which contained the safe and strong box. He knocked out the bulkhead of the cabin and was able to get the small safe up on deck — but that was as far as it got. On his previous dives he had suffered severe pain, but on this one it was even worse. He got the bends so bad that he had to be taken for medical attention. As a result of these dives, he became a cripple.

However, he eventually returned to the wreck. Putting his gear on under great pain, he dove again to the *Atlantic*'s deck, only to find that what he was looking for had disappeared. He was pulled up very distressed and again with the bends. What had happened was that another well-known diver, Elliott P. Harrington, had been there just previously and had been successful in recovering the treasure on his first dive. Green, badly bent on his last effort, ended his diving career. He spent the rest of his life full of resentment for those who had beaten him out of his supposed fortune.

Stories are still going around that when the *Atlantic* sank she had $250,000 in gold coin on board, not just the $35,000 that was reported by the authorities. If this is the case, it's still there waiting to be found.

The *Atlantic* has a strange companion resting nearby, a submarine. The inventor of the first submarine to be used on the Great Lakes, Lodner D. Philips from Michigan City, planned to use this in a possible attempt to salvage the *Atlantic* in 1864. Philips was on board his submarine when it descended to the wreck. However, it started to leak and had to be brought back to the surface. On the next attempt, the sub was lowered on a rope, but the rope parted and the vessel went to the bottom. Fortunately there was no one in the submarine at that time. Whoever locates the *Atlantic* will also be rewarded by finding a mid-nineteenth-century submarine.

In 1873 a group of adventurers decided that money could be made if they could salvage all the belongings lost by the Norwegian immigrants. To do this they were going to raise the entire vessel. This venture proved unsuccessful.

In 1953 Harry Gamble of Port Dover, with Roland Smith, Jack Holzer and Jack Maythem, planned to salvage the wreck. The divers located the ship and she was found to be in good shape. By this time the *Atlantic* had been on the bottom for over a hundred years. The crew were concerned about the equipment they were using for this depth. Not taking chances, they stopped the operation until they could come up with more satisfactory equipment. The thoughts were that a diving bell would assist in doing the job much more safely and would give them much more time to work underneath the surface. But they never returned to the *Atlantic* to continue their salvage attempt.

Another interesting development occurred concerning the *Atlantic*. Gary Kozak of Klein Assoicates, using sidescan sonar with an accompanying Klein Hydroscan system, came up with some excellent recordings of the ship. They were looking for the *Dean Richmond*, lost in 1893 with a cargo of gold bullion, copper and lead. When they came upon the *Atlantic*, the sidescan recordings plainly showed her arch, paddlewheels, walking beam and forward mast. But no divers were sent down to investigate.

In 1987 it was reported that the ill-fated *Atlantic* had been visited frequently over the past few years. However, it is my understanding that both the visitor and his endeavours wish to remain anonymous. I will respect this request.

Perhaps someday the rest of the story of the *Atlantic* will be told.

Conductor and Abigail Becker

Conductor was a two-masted topsail schooner fitted with three yards to support square sails well up on her forward mast. She could be classified as the typical type of schooner known as "The Workhorse of the Great Lakes." The vessel was owned by Mr. John McLeod of Amherstburg.

On the morning of November 23, 1854, she took on a cargo of 8,000 bushels of corn at her home port of Amherstburg. They left port early that morning and headed for Toronto via the Welland Canal. On board were Captain Henry Hackett and his crew of seven. They were on their last trip of the season. As the ship proceeded in an easterly direction, the barometer fell rapidly, gale-force winds built up and the vessel began to labour in the heavy seas. Approaching Long Point, they encountered blinding snow squalls, and the lake showed no mercy.

The captain decided to head for the Long Point cut, get through and ride out the storm on the lee side in the inner bay. Darkness set in and the raging blizzard made visibility impossible. The entrance could not be found, and they decided to sail around the end of the Point, over to the north side, and hopefully reach safe harbour. The gale-force winds blew out the sails and *Conductor* couldn't maintain course. She was constantly being pushed ashore. Driven onto a bar near the breakwater, the schooner became stranded 200 yards from shore.

With the heavy seas breaking over the hull, the staunchions starting to part, and the bulkheads twisting, it was certain she was doomed. The crew knew that if they jumped into the cold, raging surf in an attempt to get ashore, they would be washed away. The yawl had been washed overboard, so the crew all climbed and lashed themselves to the rigging. There

Artist sketch of the schooner Conductor lost November 24, 1854, near the breakwater, Long Point. — R.V. Mierlo

they perched, freezing in the blinding snowstorm. At this point they realized that their only escape from this unmerciful discomfort was death.

About a mile down the beach from where the *Conductor* was stranded, Jeremiah Becker's cabin stood. He was a trapper who lived on Long Point with his wife, Abigail, and their children. When the schooner became stranded, he was not on Long Point but had gone to the mainland to sell his pelts and buy supplies. The day he left, Mrs. Becker had misgivings about him crossing the bay in the prevailing storm conditions. The fury of the breakers gave her no rest. Her anxiety for those exposed to the fierce tempest made the night one long agony. Finally she could take this no longer, so went out on the beach to see if anyone was in distress.

Abigail Becker with the gold medal received from the New York Lifesaving Benevolent Association for saving the lives of the crew of the Conductor. — Norfolk Historical Society

The plaque in Port Rowan, overlooking the harbour, honouring The Heroine of Long Point, erected by the Ontario Archaeological and Historic Sites Board. The plaque reads as follows: "In November 1854 the schooner Conductor was wrecked off this shore during one of Lake Erie's many violent storms. Jeremiah Becker, who resided nearby, was away on the mainland but his courageous wife, Abigail, risked her life by repeatedly entering the water while assisting the exhausted seamen to reach land. The eight sailors were housed and fed in her cabin until they recovered from their ordeal. In recognition of her heroism she received a letter of commendation from Queen Victoria, several financial rewards and a gold medal from the Benevolent Association of New York. — Dave Stone

At dawn she saw the *Conductor*, fast on the bar, waves covering her hull and freezing as fast as they hit. Looking through the gloom, she spotted the crew up in the rigging. Immediately she built a huge bonfire and waved encouragement to the half-frozen sailors. Abigail Becker, six foot two and a non-swimmer, waded into the pounding surf. She encouraged the men to jump from the stricken ship, and she brought them ashore one at a time. All were taken off except the cook, who refused to leave the ship because he couldn't swim. The rescued men were warmed by the fire and then taken to the Becker cabin for food and shelter. The next morning the crew returned to the beach to find the ship's cook alive and still in the rigging. They built a raft and rescued him. He stayed at the Becker cabin until he was restored to health.

For her heroic deed Abigail Becker received a purse of $500 from the sailors, merchants and ship owners from Buffalo, as well as a gold medal struck in her hon-our from the New York Lifesaving Benevolent Association and one from the Royal Humane Society. Queen Victoria sent a letter of commendation, and congratulations were received from the Governor General of Canada, Lord Aberdeen. The Prince of Wales, later to become King Edward VII, visited her when he was hunting at Long Point and presented her with a gift. During her lifetime Mrs. Becker saved the lives of 12 persons. What a fitting title to bestow on her, "The Heroine of Long Point."

After the rescue of the crew, the *Conductor* broke up. Her spars and some rigging washed up on the beach, part of her hull became entombed in the sand, and the rest of her timbers disappeared from view.

The author with some hardware retrieved from the bottom of the inner bay.
— Dave Stone

The Mystery Schooner of Long Point Bay

The inner bay at Long Point is known as a sportsman's paradise. Surrounded mainly by marshes, it makes duck hunting renowned in Ontario. Its excellent spawning ground is ideal for large and small-mouth bass, as well as other species of fish, and make it a mecca for sport fishermen.

This body of water has on its boundaries the mainland, with St. Williams and Port Rowan to the north, Long Point causeway to the west (joining the mainland with the former island of Long Point), the open water of outer bay to the east, and to the south the Point itself, Ryerson Island, the marshes of the Long Point Company and their headquarters, the marshes of the Canadian Wildlife Service and the provincial park.

Three quarters of the inner bay are surrounded by marshes, with the exception of the two villages, Port Rowan and St. Williams, and here marinas have been established. The bottom of the bay varies from muck and silt to clear sand, from areas with minimal plant growth to others which have dense weed beds growing right to the surface. The shallow bay varies in depth from less than 2 feet to 12 feet.

The real find in the inner bay is the remains of a three-masted schooner lying in a dense weed bed. It rests in an open area on the sandy bottom in nine feet of water. Sitting on the wreck, one can observe the largest bass — which I didn't think grew that big — darting in and out of the weed bed. Moving off the

The wrecked schooner surrounded by dense weeds.
— John Veber

One of the mast steps, still in good shape. — John Veber

hull, you become entangled in the jungle of weeds that grows to the surface. The only way a diver can get oriented is to come to the top and look around for direction.

During early June 1986 a fellow diver, John Veber, one of the best underwater photographers in the area, and I took some measurements of the schooner's remains. The hull was approximately 120 feet long. Part of the bow was missing, which would account for another six to eight feet. Her width measured 23 feet amidships. There are three mast steps showing. The vessel had two centreboards, one 17½ feet, the forward one 28 feet. Both centreboards were removed and the larger one, which was brought ashore during the 1950s, is on display at Long Point. Rib ends rise several feet from the keel and planking. It's estimated that this wreck is well over 130 years old.

Due to the shallow depth where it lies, practically all artifacts have been removed, such as tongs for carrying railroad ties, joiner plates for railroad ties, padlocks, glass bottles, ink wells, ceramic bottles, a lid from a woodburning Van Norman woodstove, and part of a pump. A large anchor was found not far from the wreck, with the chain with a broken link pointing to the wreck. This could have been one of her anchors.

To the immediate west of the wreckage, approximately a quarter of a mile, is another piece of wreckage 35 feet in length. Tom Backus of Port Rowan and Mervin Hicks of Tillsonburg located the wreck in the mid-1950s. Hicks spotted it from his plane and directed Backus to the area where the schooner lay.

There are a number of different stories concerning this wreckage, but the evidence to date is inconclusive. The old-timers in the area say it's the *George McCall*, which sunk at anchor in 1906. The *McCall*, a small wooden schooner, carried cargo in this vicinity for many years. Some historians feel that she was not as large a vessel as the one lying in the weed bed. However, perhaps the small bit of wreckage west of the other wreck could be her bones.

During the early 1970s Chris Blythe, a diver and student at Georgian College, did some research on the wreck. His thoughts at that time were that she was a two-master. From the appearance, he thought there

The larger centreboard at Long Point off the mystery schooner.
— Dave Stone

Anchor off the schooner, now located on a front lawn in Port Rowan. — Dave Stone

could have been a fire on board that burned it to the waterline. The wood is definitely black on some parts of the vessel, but age may also be the cause. She was built for shallow water and was possibly hauling logs to the sawmill at Port Royal. Back in the early days, a vessel such as this would have had no trouble sailing up Big Creek to its destination. Blythe figured a squall caught her and washed her aground on Whitefish Bar. He concluded that after she went aground she was set on fire to collect the insurance. His talks with local inhabitants revealed nothing but speculation. However, despite this, he was one of the first to attempt an in-depth study of the remains of this old vessel.

During 1986 a diving buddy of mine, John Veber, became curious about the wreck. He decided to do some intensive research, hoping he could come up with some concrete evidence as to the vessel's identification.

He came across the name of a schooner called *Ontario*, length 133 feet, width 23 feet, with three masts and a gross tonnage of 338 tons. She was built in Quebec City in 1851 by A. St. Jean, and the original owner was merchant David Gilmour of Quebec City. In March 1856 the vessel came under the ownership of Henry Waters, a lumber merchant from Chatham. On Monday, August 30, 1858, the following report was given in the *Marine News*. The schooner *Star of Hope* came into Port Colborne with the crew from the *Ontario*, nine men and a woman. They had spent seven hours in the rigging of the waterlogged schooner off Long Point, caught in a sudden squall. The tug *Underwriter* went out to look for the *Ontario* but found only some pieces of wreckage and some square timbers. The tug returned to Port Colborne presuming she had gone to pieces. She was reported lost on the north shore near Long Point.

There are several factors to consider. *Ontario*'s measurements were about the same as those of the mystery wreck. She was carrying lumber and lumbering tools found on the wreck. And, she was one of the few lost on the north shore near Long Point.

This does not solve the mystery of the inner bay wreck, but knowing my friend John Veber, with his determination, he will someday come up with something that will identify the lost schooner.

The first recorded wreck on the Point was the schooner *Young Phoenix*, on September 14, 1818. Since that date there has been a long list of lost ships, people and cargoes. However, the wreck list does not tell the whole story. What about the number of vessels that the fury of Long Point waters have brought to *near* disaster. These are the ones that were blown ashore in gales but were able to be repaired and sail again on the Great Lakes.

Many things happened to vessels off Long Point besides total wreckage. There were those that survived collisions, others that capsized but were righted and put in service again. A ship losing her anchors and becoming stranded on a bar was not uncommon. Some of these had the good fortune to be refloated once the storm subsided. Ships' hulls have been so badly pounded by the cruel wave action that seams have opened up. in some cases the pumps saved these from ending up in the Graveyard of the Great Lakes. Other ships became demasted but were able to ride out the huge waves until the lake ceased its anger and they could be towed into a safe harbour for repairs. Then there were the steamers that received engine damage due to the violent seas. These too were repaired once the waters had calmed and they could be towed into port. Some ships got caught in the ice but had the good fortune to be released before they were crushed. Fire is the terror which all seamen fear. It can be started by the carelessness of the crew, a red hot clinker from the galley stove or the boiler room, or in some cases by lightning. The ships that survived fires on board were saved through the vigorous efforts of captains and crews who wouldn't let fire get the upper hand. A vessel could be badly damaged but still stay afloat.

The amount of property damage that the Point and its waters have caused is overwhelming. Damaged vessels greatly outnumber those that became total losses. The following list for the ten-year period 1858 to 1868 shows the number of vessels that received damage but survived to sail again. This ten-year period was not the peak decade for wrecks. The peak occurred from 1870 to 1880, because during this period there were many more ships and the storms were more intense. Sailing vessels still prevailed, but they were very vulnerable to the fierce storms off Long Point.

Month	Vessel	What Happened	Property Damage
		1858	
April	Sloop	Capsized	150
April	Brig. John Young	Capsized, cargo stoves	8,000
June	Sch. Danon	Collision	80
July	Prop. Mayflower	Collision	500
August	Sch. Lookout	Ashore on Long Point	1,000
September	Sch. Elk	Ashore, threw over 25 tons coal	100
October	Sch. Andover	Lost anchors and chains	500
October	Sch. J.C. Fremont	Ashore above Long Point Cut	2,100
October	Barque Sir E. Mead	Lost anchor, chain & boat	1,300
October	Sch. Watchful	Lost anchor and chain	100
			$13,830

Month	Vessel	What Happened	Property Damage
		1859	
September	Sch. Cascade	Ashore, damaged cargo	200
September	Sch. Comelia	Ashore, cargo lost, grain	12,000
September	Prop. King	Collision	1,000
October	Prop. Iona	Machinery, disabled	100
October	Sch. J. Cochrane	Damaged in a gale	1,700
			$15,000
		1860	
April	Brig. Globe	Damaged by collision	200
July	Sch. Storm	Ashore, cargo lost	4,700
September	Sch. Eliza Logan	Dismasted, towed to Buffalo	1,050
September	Sch. Philena Mills	Ashore	200
October	Sch. T.G. Scott	Ashore	2,000
November	Sch. Kenocka	Collision	700
			$8,850
		1861	
August	Sch. C.J. Rocdor	Collision	800
September	Prop. Santa	Collision	400
			$1,200
		1862	
May	Prop. Detroit	Machinery broken in gale	500
August	Sch. Gertrude	Collision	500
October	Sch. Luddington	Ashore	2,500
November	Prop. Plymouth	Ashore, lost cargo, corn and flour	4,300
November	Brig. Commerce	Ashore, cargo coal	11,000
			$18,800
		1864	
July	Sch. Commerce	Waterlogged, reached Buffalo	2,000
October	Sch. Comely	Badly damaged	800
November	Sch. Homeward Bound	Lost anchors	200
			$3,000
		1865	
May	Barque H.H. Brown	Ashore	250
November	Brig. William Treat	Ashore, cargo wheat	1,000
			$1,250

Month	Vessel	What Happened	Property Damage
		1863	
April	Sch. Miami Belle	Ashore, cargo wheat	2,750
May	Sch. J.L. Reid	Collision	1,000
June	Sch. L.A. Marsh	Collision	120
October	Prop. Eclipse	Collision	150
October	Sch. Monteagle	Ashore, cargo lost, wheat	16,000
October	Sch. Elk	Cargo damaged, wheat	100
October	Sch. Linnie Powell	Cargo damaged	100
November	Prop. Magnet	Ashore	1,300
November	Barque Mary Jane	Ashore, cargo wheat	12,000
November	Sch. Storm Spirit	Demasted in gale	12,333
			$45,853
		1866	
July	Sch. Black Hawk	Lost sails, Long Point Cut	180
July	Barque Maitland	Lost mainsail, Long Point Cut	200
August	Sch. S. Morton	Damaged sails	150
October	Barque Camer	Lost deckload of lumber	800
			$1,330
		1867	
July	Sch. Akron	Collision	200
July	Sch. Acont	Collision	300
September	Sch. Ian Jacinto	Ashore at Long Point Cut, cargo grain	3,000
			$3,500
		1868	
March	Prop. H. Howard	Damaged in ice	300
April	Barque Annie Sherwood	Ashore, cargo grain	200
July	Sch. Monteray	Ashore	500
September	Barque Grace Greenwood	Ashore, cargo grain	2,000
October	Prop. Tonawanda	Collision	250
			$3,250

Abbreviations   Sch. Schooner   Prop.| Propeller Steamer   Brig. Brigantine

For the above period, 1858 to 1868, there were 55 vessels (45 sail, 10 steamers) that received some form of damage while sailing in the Long Point area. The dollar value for damages suffered was $115, 863. Also, during this same period, there were 26 vessels that were a complete loss (21 sail, 5 steamers) on and off Long Point. Information obtained from Public Works records, Public Archives of Canada, Ottawa, Ont. Loss of life and property on Lake Erie, Canadian side 1858-1868.

This was probably the thought going through Captain Nickerson's mind as he sat in the yawl boat with 14 other survivors from his crew. If they had stayed in Gravelly Bay, Long Point, for a longer period, and his command had blown up then, they would at least have been close to shore and been rescued by members of the Long Point lifesaving station. Of course at that time he had no idea what was going to happen to his ship.

But here they were now, 30 miles west of Long Point and 10 miles from land, their yawl drifting aimlessly in the lake in the cold November weather. One minute there had been a ship and the next very little of the vessel remained above water, just the hurricane deck and her bow.

This is what happened to the 11-year-old wooden propeller steamer *Ohio*. She was a double-decker with a single mast and round stern. At the time of her loss the 159-foot steamer was owned by the American Transportation Company. She had left Buffalo with a 350-ton cargo bound for Cleveland. It was early November 1859. She encountered a typical November storm en route, so put in for shelter at Gravelly Bay, Long Point. There she stayed until the waters on the south shore of the point settled down, then continued on course for Cleveland. The weather was good and the steamer was making good progress. When *Ohio* was approximately 30 miles above the Point, the captain decided to retire. He had only been in his bunk ten minutes when the ship blew up. Scrambling up on the deck, he saw very little of the ship left and his crew jumping overboard.

Both the steamer's yawl boats were blown into the water. One fortunately landed right side up and 15 of the 17-member crew climbed on board. Lost were the second mate and the other wheelsman.

The 14-year-old son of the captain had come along this trip, and if it hadn't been for the efforts of one crew member, it would have been his last voyage. When the vessel exploded, the young lad's cabin fell right into the lake, trapping him inside. One of the engineers reached under the cabin and pulled him out.

In the yawl, the men, with hardly any clothes, nearly perished from the cold. At one point they spotted two vessels, which raised their hopes of being rescued. However, these ships did not see them and passed by. In the turbulent waters and cold November winds the crew were weakening and some had given up hope.

As the day turned to evening the propeller steamer *Equator* heard their cries of distress. They were picked up approximately 15 miles from land, given comfort and medical attention, and all of the 15 survived this ordeal.

Why the *Ohio* blew up no one knows. Just before the explosion, an engineer had said the machinery sounded in good working order, and a fireman had just checked the boiler water, which was satisfactory. The *Ohio* had a value listed at $15,000 and was uninsured.

Explosions on the lake were not rare. Periodically a ship would simply blow up, with no ship or survivors to explain why!

The approximate area on Long Point where the crew members of the Jersey City were found in their gruesome positions of death.

Jersey City — Death on the Beach at Long Point

The *Jersey City* was built by George W. Jones in 1855 at Cleveland, Ohio. Its owners were the New York & Erie Railroad Company of New York. This propeller steamer was 182 feet long and had a gross tonnage of 633 tons. Her career was short. Five years after her launching she foundered off Long Point.

On November 25, 1860, she left the port of Buffalo bound for Toledo with a crew of 20 and two passengers. her cargo consisted of flour, pork and a deckload of cattle for the stockyards. The weather upon leaving Buffalo was not the best but was typical for late November and did not appear to hold any great danger. But as their journey progressed conditions got worse.

As they neared the end of Long Point the ship was plunging into heavy seas. Some of the cattle were washed overboard. Gale-force winds sent destructive waves boarding the vessel. Although well built, the *Jersey City* couldn't continue to take the relentless pounding. Her seams started to open up, and soon the rising water put her fires out. at this point a large wave washed completely over her, taking one of the passengers with it. The body was located much later, washed up on the beach on the north side of Long Point. The

The Jersey City's sternpost reared itself heavenward in this vicinity. Could this bit of wreckage uncovered by high water be part of the Jersey City?

Jersey City, driven ashore by the enormous waves, was still just barely afloat. The crew decided to try for the beach. All made it ashore except one crew member, who was washed overboard as he attempted to launch the yawl.

By this time a snow squall had blown up in full force, and once the survivors reached shore they had no place to go for shelter. The *Jersey City* had come to rest a few miles from the lighthouse. In the panic and confusion that followed, some started going down the beach one way, others the other way. They did not know where they had come ashore. Some just stayed a short distance from where they had landed, and died of exposure.

The two engineers were found frozen to death 300 yards from the lighthouse. Others were found in gruesome positions: sitting ·on logs, crouched behind bushes, several embracing each other in death. The body of the black cook was found the next spring leaning against a tree some distance from the lighthouse.

The captain, the wheelsman, two engineers and one passenger were the only ones who made it to the light-house. They suffered from severe frostbite but recovered. Out of 22, five were left to tell the story. What an awesome sight it must have been for Harry Clark, the lighthouse keeper, when he went down the beach to investigate the loss. Clark spent over 25 years of his life keeping the Long Point light, but never again would he see such a sight of horror as this.

Some salvage attempts were made on this ill-fated ship. One report states that during the 1860s Captain Dan Munroe, Sandusky, Ohio, recovered a valuable copper boiler. This eventually ended up in an American gunboat which served throughout the Civil War. It was also reported that in 1861 some of the *Jersey City*'s machinery was salvaged and taken to Port Dover by the schooners *Ada* and *L.C. Butts*.

For some time the sternpost still reared itself heavenward near Anderson's Pond. This silent monument was there as a reminder to all who passed. Its message: "Take heed of the late-fall Lake Erie storms or you too will perish like the *Jersey City* and the members of her crew."

Pocahontas ran aground on Long Point on April 8, 1862, to keep from sinking.

Pocohontas

The *Pocahontas* was built in Buffalo, New York, in 1846 by Frederick W. Jones. This wooden propeller steamer was 171¾ feet in length. She had a gross tonnage of 126 tons. Her ports of call were Cleveland, Sandusky, Toledo, Detroit and Buffalo. Her owner was the American Transportation Company of Buffalo.

In the early spring of 1862 she steamed from Buffalo with a cargo of corn and flour bound for Toledo. Somewhere off Long Point she began taking on water in her hull. The leak couldn't be stopped and the pumps couldn't keep ahead of the lake coming in. The decision was made to run her aground on the inside of Long Point. Under a head of steam she made for the beach and ran aground. The crew were saved, but the vessel and cargo were lost. The *Pocahontas* broke up and her timbers reached their final disposition, scattered the length of Long Point.

Pocahontas, like other vessels before her, had sought the comfort and safety of Long Point's outstretched arm only to be destroyed once in its clutches.

Section of the marsh at Long Point where the remains of a schooner were located.
— Dave Stone

Rebecca Foster — The Ship that Travelled Overland

On June 5, 1857, Captain David Montague Foster launched the 90-ton schooner *Rebecca Foster* from his Port Rowan shipyard. He named this stout little schooner after his oldest child.

Captain Foster was a well-known shipbuilder, and his schooners and steamers had the reputation of being the best on the lakes. He had shipyards operating in Port Burwell and Port Rowan between 1852 and 1880. He was in partnership with Major Ryerse of Port Ryerse in a yard there from 1860 to 1864. While there he built several ships. He had other shipyards in Flint and Reed Lake, Michigan, and at Reed Lake he built a 1,000-ton passenger excursion steamer. As another phase of his business, Foster operated excursion boats from Port Burwell to Port Dover. From 1888 to 1905, at London, Ontario, he built two excursion pleasure boats used on the Thames River, running out of Springbank Park. In total he built 45 vessels, mainly schooners but some steamers. These sailed the entire Great Lakes system, and one even made it across the ocean.

The schooner *Rebecca Foster* was known as a well-built ship, and she encountered many bad storms during her lifetime and handled them with little difficulty.

50

She worked her way up and down the lakes, carrying everything from barrel staves to beef carcasses. The vessel was owned by Laycock and Davis before her loss.

During the late fall of 1863 she encountered a storm that swept Lake Erie with unbelievable force, and it caught the schooner off the Cut at Long Point. She was trying to make the channel so shelter could be obtained in the bay when her sails blew out. She was left wallowing helplessly in the heavy seas, with the southwest gale hitting her broadside. There was fear that she was going to capsize.

Suddenly, as the gale strengthened, mountainous rollers swept the ship up on the beach. These huge rollers followed one after another. The ship was floating on what had previously been dry land. The huge waves continued to roll in, and they carried the schooner overland and deposited her on the bay side. The *Rebecca Foster* had travelled across Long Point without the assistance of the Cut.

The saying is that lightning doesn't strike twice in the same place. Well it did. The very next year, 1864, the same thing happened to the schooner *Sam Amsden*. These two shipwrecks contributed to the total number of 31 off the Cut at Long Point between 1833 and 1906.

The *Rebecca Foster* was so badly damaged, she was abandoned where she came to rest. The remains of the *Sam Amsden* were salvaged, with the exception of her masts and rigging.

One hundred years later, some well-preserved oak timbers from the frame of a schooner were found on the bay side of Long Point. They were found in the vicinity on the former Cut and in about the same area where the schooners travelled overland.

Square-sided nails protruded from the timbers used to fasten the planking to the ship's frame. Some timbers, placed end to end, formed the ship's ribs. A framework section fastened together looked like part of the bow structure.

The remains of the vessel were uncovered from a depth of five feet when a dragline struck them while digging a boat channel. Unfortunately these were never looked at by anyone who knew ship construction and could give positive identification as to the ship's vintage, so there is no definite proof that it is the *Rebecca Foster*. However, to the best of my knowledge, it is the only one that ended up in this area.

Little did Captain David Foster realize on June 5, 1857, that his schooner would spend eternity somewhere in the marsh at Long Point.

Prior to the operation of the Long Point lifesaving station, there was never any readily available help to assist a ship in distress offshore. The lives of those on an ill-fated vessel depended on whether there was a volunteer crew ashore available to assist them in their plight.

Such was the case of the *Jennie P. King*, a 145-foot American three-masted barque. She had been built in Tonawanda, New York, in 1863 for $16,000. At the time of her loss, she still belonged to the original owner, D. Van Valekenburg of Lockport, New York.

The three-year-old vessel met her end on June 18, 1866. She had a cargo of oak timbers on board and had sailed from Toledo, destination Tonawanda.

Early that afternoon off Long Point, the barque *King* encountered one of Long Point's many violent storms with gale-force winds. Timber-carrying ships were usually not the best class of ship, but the *Jennie P. King* had the distinction of being a first-class vessel and was built to take what punishment the lakes had to offer.

On this day the ship found herself in giant waves, which crashed over her decks and carried the vessel well over on its side after each pounding. With part of her cargo on deck, she struggled every time to right herself. Eventually she was hit by the last great wave she would ever encounter. It turned the barque completely over, and 13 of the 14 passengers and crew were lost.

Captain Edward Quinn shouted words of hope to those who were clinging to the lower section of the rigging, but they were unable to climb higher and so were lost. One passenger fell from the rigging and landed on the captain, knocking him off his perch. He fell into the foaming sea, never to be seen again.

The schooner *Egyptian* tried to assist the stricken *King*, but this was impossible due to the violent waters.

Hours later the vessel drifted ashore at the Old Cut, her fore and main masts broken, leaving only the mizzen. Still on board, the one survivor, Thomas McGinnis, clung to the crosstrees.

Back on shore William Woodard — a distant relative of my wife — gathered a crew together in Port Rowan and sailed for Long Point. Battling giant combers, Woodard's boat nearly capsized several times before they reached the barque. With great difficulty they managed to remove McGinnis and get him safely to shore.

This dangerous rescue would be repeated many times by volunteers, who time and time again risked their lives to aid those in distress. It wasn't until 1883 that the first lifesaving station was built on Long Point and manned with a captain and seven oarsmen. The location of this station was on the south beach, west of the Old Cut lighthouse. After the fall of 1883, stricken sailors no longer had to have their lives saved by chance, waiting for a volunteer crew to be made up so they could be saved.

Empire as a sidewheel passenger steamer, once the largest ship in the world.

Empire

The wooden sidewheel steamer *Empire* was built at Cleveland, Ohio, by George W. Jones in 1844. The vessel was 253½ feet long and had a breadth of 32⅔ feet. At the time of launching, June 5, 1844, *Empire* was the largest ship in the world, with a gross tonnage of 1,140 tons. Her two inclined high-pressure engines, with a cylinder and stroke of 45x10, were built by Cuyahoga Steam Furnace Company. *Empire* operated as a passenger steamer until 1865. She was a fast ship and could run from Detroit to Buffalo in 21½ hours.

By 1859 the demand for the larger passenger steamers was fading away, and the railroads had taken over the transportation of passengers and freight. From 1852 to 1864 *Empire* was owned by the Michigan Southern Railway Company and was still being used as a passenger steamer. In 1865 she was completely rebuilt and converted to a steam barge. She was slightly lengthened, to 255 feet, but her gross tonnage fell to 702 tons. The appearance of the ship was changed completely. Her engines and sidewheels were removed and major alterations were made to the upper decks. When the refit was completed at Detroit, she had become a propeller steam barge.

On November 12, 1870, the *Empire* left Port Huron with a cargo of lumber and shingles bound for Buffalo. Nearing Long Point she sprang a leak. She was run aground about a mile from the Long Point Cut. A short time after striking land, she started to go to pieces under the continuous pounding of the November rollers. The crew of 14 made rafts from the cargo and, after a narrow escape, drifted safely to shore. Once they landed, the stricken *Empire* broke up, spewing her cargo of lumber and shingles all along the beach, much to the delight of future scavengers.

At the time of her loss, the ship belonged to Thomas and John McGregor of Detroit and was under American registration.

On October 15, 1877, three vessels were caught in one of Long Point's notorious late-fall storms and were driven up on the south beach.

The *British Lion*, a large brig owned by a Mr. Dawson of Kent, was the first. The vessel was valued at $20,000 and in her hold was a cargo of 400 tons of coal. She was bound for Buffalo when she ran aground. She hit the beach with such violent force that it broke her back. She was a total loss to her owner, as he carried no insurance on the vessel or the cargo.

The second vessel to be lost that day was the schooner *Madeira*, with a cargo of 22,000 bushels of wheat on board. She hailed from Milwaukee and was bound for Buffalo.

She lay at anchor for some time, her rudder was gone and she wallowed helplessly in the raging surf. Some of the crew decided to try to go ashore to obtain another rudder, but the heavy seas would not permit them to launch a yawl safely. Violent waves tore over the schooner's deck, and the crew decided to slip the pin on the anchor cable and let the *Madeira* drift ashore. She ran aground on the beach a short distance from the *British Lion* and filled with water.

The next vessel was the 425-ton schooner *Eliza A. Turner*. She had picked up her 27,000 bushels of wheat at Cleveland and she too was sailing to Buffalo. The vessel was overloaded and could not take the punishment that was being applied to her hull. She began to ship more water than what would run off and soon became waterlogged.

The first mate, realizing she was going to sink, set his course for the beach. The vessel ran aground about a quarter of a mile from the *British Lion* and the *Madeira*.

Just before the *Eliza A. Turner* went aground, the captain, who was also the owner, went below to his cabin to get $800 he had stashed away. As he left the cabin a large wave washed him overboard. The same wave took a female cook, and they both went to their watery graves.

The ten crew members still on board climbed into the rigging and stayed there for 35 hours. The seas finally settled down, and they were able to get safely off the grounded schooner and onto the beach.

The cargoes of wheat on the *Madeira* and the *Eliza A. Turner* were insured for $60,000. When the underwriters arrived, the wrecks were lined up on the beach, spaced so evenly that it looked as if some giant hand had placed them there. Tugs, steam pumps and all the necessary equipment were lined up to help save their cargoes, but as the cargoes were all insured in the United States, the Canadian authorities would not allow them to carry on this operation. Because none of the necessary equipment was available on this side of the border the stricken vessels were left to their doom, and the cargoes of wheat were scattered up and down the beach.

The captain and cook's bodies were located about three weeks after the drownings. No money was found on the captain; the only thing of value was his watch.

This one day, October 15, 1877, proved how helpless ships are when they are caught in the "killer storms" that sweep Long Point in the late fall.

*The Ghost of Long Point
looking for his severed head.
— Julia Stone*

The Ghost of Long Point

Where there are shipwrecks there are always ghosts! Long Point is no exception to this folklore. The location is a perfect setting for a haunting — stretches of bogs and swamps oozing their way through a wilderness of weedy quills, sand dunes moulded by gales into eerie shapes, trees contorted by the November storms, twisting them into fearsome shapes that would terrify anyone during a full moon, the white sandy beaches scattered with the remains of once proud vessels and the tombs of shipwrecked victims.

One November night in the 1880s, a steamer with a crew of 14 downbound for the Welland Canal was caught in a fierce gale mid-length of Long Point. The ship, loaded with a cargo of coal, laboured helplessly as the huge waves broke over her bow. As the punishing rollers smashed against the ship, pieces of the upper deck were demolished and disappeared into the surging foam.

The captain, realizing his ship was breaking up, headed for the beach at Long Point. The moon was full and they could see the outline of the shore, with the booming surf and the white-capped breakers waiting to devour them. In the background could be seen the gloomy forests, with the dead trees stretching their bonelike branches upward like fingers beckoning them to come within their grasp.

The Ghost's pet, found on Long Point. — Dave Stone

As the vessel steamed towards the beach, the crew were terror-stricken. They knew the ship was breaking up so fast they would never reach the shore. The captain ordered the lifeboat swung out. They all scrambled aboard, but in their haste to lower the boat, the head of one seaman became caught in the davit. As the boat dropped, his head was severed from his body and fell overboard. The crew screamed in terror, but they managed to get the boat ashore, with the headless seaman on board.

They began to search along the beach for the missing head. Unsuccessful, they waited for the pounding surf to wash it ashore. They eventually realized they would have to bury the unfortunate seaman without his head. Sadly they performed this task and then walked the beach to safety.

Over the years this story has been told and retold. If a doubter will go a mile east of the breakwater when the moon is full, he'll see the headless seaman walking the beach, looking for his severed head.

Erie Wave — The Schooner with a Jonah

There were some ships in the early days on the Great Lakes that the old-time sailors said were jinxed, vessels that were known for their misfortunes, time and time again, causing loss of life and property. These ships had difficulty getting crews to man them or shippers to entrust their cargoes to them. The *Erie Wave* was known as one of these ships, and she was finally lost near Long Point during the late 1860s.

On her very first voyage she was caught in a violent blow, her sails couldn't be lowered fast enough and she turned over. Two members of the crew were washed away from the overturned vessel and disappeared from sight. According to reports, the bodies of these hapless sailors were never recovered.

The schooner was salvaged, repaired and put back into service. On her next trip she ran into a squall and over she went again, taking the lives of two passengers with her.

Once more *Erie Wave* was repaired, and on her last voyage she blew ashore near Long Point. She got off again that same night a gale caught the schooner and rolled her over on a bar between Port Rowan and Clear Creek, where the waves broke her up. The passengers and crew couldn't scramble to safety without fear of drowning. Two finally made it to the beach, but the rest of the crew and passengers drowned. The bodies came ashore near the Old Cut, and from there were taken into Port Rowan.

Many years later the sailors still spoke of the *Erie Wave*, "The Schooner with a Jonah" or "The Bad Luck Boat."

William H. Vanderbilt

On a bar on the south shore, near the Old Cut, Long Point, the 169-foot three-masted schooner *William H. Vanderbilt* neared her end. The fatal day was September 24, 1883. She had left Escanaba, Michigan, bound for Buffalo with her hold full of iron ore. As she neared Long Point, she became trapped in the fury of one of the lake's fall storms. She was soon driven ashore, her sails torn to ribbons. The *Vanderbilt* was at the complete mercy of the waves.

The crew of nine, realizing the ship was in danger of breaking up, sought shelter in the tattered rigging. Their plight was spotted from shore, but the only way they could be saved was for someone to get a boat out to them through the foaming surf. The lifesaving station had recently been commissioned and the station boat was available, but no permanent crew had been appointed.

Captain Crocker, an experienced sailor who had been through an ordeal like this before, picked a crew. The lifeboat was launched and they headed for the distressed schooner to offer assistance, with the surf running so high they too were in danger of swamping. Finally, after great difficulty, they reached the *William H. Vanderbilt*, lying in 15 feet of water with her cargo of iron ore still on board. The crew were in an exhausted condition in the tattered rigging. But they were all safely taken off, leaving their personal effects on board. The captain lost some personal papers, a gold watch and $300.

After the captain and crew were landed on the beach, they could not find the words to express their gratitude to the crew of the lifeboat. They realized that if they had not been taken off at that moment, they would have perished. It was the brave skill and management of the lifesaving crew that had saved them.

The crew of the *William H. Vanderbilt* left the abandoned schooner to her fate and returned to the comfort of their homes. By a stroke of good fortune the captain's personal papers and money came ashore less than a month after the vessel was lost. These were found on the beach by William Dickenson not too far from the wreck. Dickenson, keeper of the Old Cut lighthouse, returned the articles to the captain, much to his delight.

About a year later, attempts were made to salvage the *Vanderbilt*. Wreckers, using the schooner *Louise* from Buffalo, removed a hundred tons of iron ore. They also got the *Vanderbilt*'s steering gear, what was left of the sails, and some anchors and chain. When the salvagers returned to the wreck site three years later in 1887, the hull had moved from 15 feet of water to 26 feet. They were able to salvage another 200 tons of iron ore.

The 520-ton *William H. Vanderbilt* started her career when she was launched in 1867 at East Saginaw, Michigan, by her builder S.J. Tripp. When she was lost, the 16-year-old schooner belonged to S.L. Watson of Buffalo, New York.

Siberia steam-screw propeller steamer, built 1882. — Great Lakes Historical Society

Don't Name Your Ship Siberia and Sail in Long Point Waters

There were two vessels on Long Point with the distinction of the name *Siberia*. One a three-masted schooner/barge lost in 1883, the other a wooden steamer lost in 1905. The schooner's bones were scattered on the south shore beach near the Old Cut lighthouse. The remains of the steamer lie in a silt bed off the north shore of Long Point. The crews of each vessel were saved by members of the Long Point lifesaving station.

The three-masted schooner/barge *Siberia* left Toledo, Ohio, with a cargo of timbers, one female passenger, two horses and a crew of nine. She was built during 1874, had Canadian registry and her home port was Kingston. Near Long Point, on October 30, 1883, running in thick weather, she became

waterlogged. It was impossible to pump the water out fast enough, and those on board were in danger of drowning. She had lost most of her sails, and there was no way the crew could navigate in such turbulent waters. The vessel finally became stranded on a bar near the Old Cut.

The crew waited on board, hoping to be saved by the members of the lifesaving station, but because of the huge breakers the lifesaving crew were unable to launch the lifeboat immediately. They had to wait until the surf settled down before they could reach the wreck. All of the crew and the one passenger were taken off safely. The only casualty was one of the horses, which was lost in the surf. William Dickenson,

Site off Long Point where the sinking occurred. — Dave Stone

keeper of the Old Cut lighthouse, and his wife took the survivors into their home, gave them dry clothing, food and shelter, and made arrangements to get them off Long Point.

The next day salvagers attempted to get the schooner afloat, but found it impossible. *Siberia* was abandoned, and it wasn't long before the elements scattered her bones up and down the south shore of Long Point.

In a silt bed southeast of the Bluffs are the remains of the second *Siberia*, a 272-foot wooden, propeller steamer. Under 21 feet of water is an assortment of timbers from the wreck — broken deck planking, beams, a portion of a hull — and machinery. These are scattered 200 feet in every direction across the silty bottom. The boiler stands upright and can be seen from the surface when the visibility is good. The *Siberia* was blown up by salvagers using dynamite during the 1960s.

This *Siberia* was built by James Davidson of West Bay City, Michigan, and was launched on June 26, 1882. After 21 years of service, she was rebuilt to increase her cargo capacity. Her home port was Fairport, Ohio, and she was owned by John W. Moore.

On October 21, 1905, the *Siberia* left Duluth, Minnesota, bound for Buffalo with a cargo óf 91,000 bushels of barley in her hold. She started to leak off Long Point and hit the Bluff Bar. The crew was taken to

59

Heath Stone holding the nameplate which washed ashore after Siberia broke up. — Dave Stone

Siberia's firebox, still intact. — John Veber

Scotch boiler and part of the hull. — John Veber

Part of Siberia's hull sitting in a silt bed. — John Veber

safety by members of the Long Point lifesaving station. *Siberia* was left stranded. Salvage operations were planned, but storm conditions changed this. In less than a week the end came for the *Siberia*. Storm conditions battered the ship to pieces, resulting in a total loss of $71,000 to vessel and cargo.

Due to poor visibility and silt conditions, *Siberia* is seldom visited. The only company she has are the mud puppies, which make the murky bottom and the fractured hull their home, and the *Pascal P. Pratt*, which lies a short distance away.

The type of seas that overcame the yawl boat of the Edmund Fitzgerald that fatal day in November 1883. — Dave Stone

Edmund Fitzgerald

What is a story about the *Edmund Fitzgerald* doing in a book about Long Point shipwrecks? We all know that the "Big Fitz," a 729-foot lake freighter was lost with all hands on November 10, 1975, in Lake Superior. However, the early gales of November also took another *Edmund Fitzgerald*, a 135-foot schooner, and a crew of eight to their end off Long Point on November 14, 1883. The vessel was built by Fitzgerald and Leighton at Port Huron, Michigan, in 1870. She was named after one of her builders. At the time of her demise the schooner belonged to a Mr. John Haley of Buffalo, New York.

On her last trip she sailed from Detroit with a cargo of wheat bound for Buffalo. The unfortunate vessel became stranded not far offshore, near the Long Point Cut lighthouse. Nearby was the Long Point lifesaving station, so it seemed the crew was in no danger and would be immediately rescued. However, it was not to be. The new captain of the station, when he heard of the disaster, rushed to the scene of the wreck, leaving the boathouse locked and the key in his pocket. When the lifesaving crew arrived at the boathouse, they found it locked. They had to force the door, put the boat on a wagon and head up the beach to the ship-wreck. There they met the captain, who informed them they were too late and that all of the *Fitzgerald* crew had drowned. After waiting for help, which failed to arrive shortly, they took to their own small boat in a desperate attempt to get ashore. The large combers soon swamped the boat. They were all lost close to shore and within sight of a number of people who were unable to help them.

It is more than likely that they all would have been saved if they had waited for the station boat, but at times of panic there is little reasoning.

For the next several days the lifeboat went out to the

wrecked schooner, dragging for the bodies of the crew with no success. The lifesaving crew also boarded the stricken vessel and reported that she was breaking up fast.

A week passed by and still no bodies had been found, even though a diligent search had been made. Eventually the battered vessel washed ashore. A gentleman from Port Colborne, a Mr. Smith, purchased the cargo of wheat for $250. This he sold for 30 cents a bag. Teams from 30 miles away came to buy the wheat. A contract was let to Dease and Stearns to salvage the schooner. They were only able to obtain one of her anchors, chain and some rigging before a storm came up and it became impossible for them to continue. It was at this point that the schooner began to break up and the remains of the cargo of wheat was washed away.

About a month after the wreck, a body was found washed up on the beach at Long Point. It was identified as Charles Bingham of Norwich, Ontario, a member of the crew.

The final disposition of this vessel was that some of her bones were scattered along the breadth of the sandy beach and the rest of her washed back out in the lake.

Even today one can see a frame, deck stanchions, keelson and other ship's timbers scattered on the beach, especially after a big storm. One wonders, are these the remains of the *Edmund Fitzgerald* or those of one of the numerous wrecks before and after her? No one will ever know except the ghosts of the crew.

The Gale of '93

A northwest gale that struck the lakes on October 14 and 15, 1893, was one of the most destructive in many years. Sixty-mile-an-hour winds were responsible for taking 41 lives, destroying 2 ships and leaving 29 stranded. One of the destroyed ships was the 250-foot wooden steam *Wocoken*, built in 1880 by Thomas Quayle and Son, Cleveland, Ohio. In command was Captain Albert Meswald, also part owner of the $65,000 vessel. Prior to her sailing from Ashtabula, she had taken on a cargo of coal. The captain's orders were to sail from Ashtabula on October 14, meet with the schooner *Joseph Paige* off Erie, and then proceed with his cargo to Milwaukee, Wisconsin.

The two vessels were caught in a gale and headed for Long Point to seek shelter in the Cut. The *Wocoken* cut the towline to the *Paige*, and under a full head of steam proceeded on her way. The violent pounding she took in the gale broke her rudder stem and water entered her hull. The steam lines were severed and her boilers flooded. The *Wocoken* went to the bottom in 50 feet of water. Captain Meswald, chief engineer Michael Hinkelman and 12 of the crew found a watery grave. The three survivors of the *Wocoken* were saved by the crew of the Long Point lifesaving station. When she went to the bottom, west of the Point, her masts protruded out of the water and supplied a perch for the three men to cling to. They were in the rigging for five hours before being rescued.

The next fall, the Michigan Salvage Company had great expectations of raising the *Wocoken*. However, when they reached the wreck site, they discovered the vessel so badly damaged that it was of little value. The boilers, steering apparatus, some of the engine and various parts of machinery were salvaged. Some of the cargo of coal was brought up, but most of it remained scattered on the bottom of the wreck.

The relentless storms of Long Point had harvested another victim.

Island Queen, "The Patchwork Hooker of Long Point Bay," built 1885-87.
— Capt. Steve Peer

Island Queen — The Floating Wreck of Long Point

The most unsightly little schooner that ever sailed in Long Point waters was the *Island Queen*. A Mr. Smith of Port Rowan built her over a three-year period, from 1895 to 1897. It didn't take three years because he was a skilled craftsman who wanted the vessel to be perfect, but because this was the time it took to gather up all the materials to put her together. He gave little thought to the quality of the wood that went into the construction, as long as it was wood.

He gathered a great deal of the materials from the wreck-strewn beach of the south shore of Long Point.

He also salvaged planking and timbers inland from fallen down buildings. Consequently the hull was made up of white oak, white ash, elm, swamp elm, pine, cherry, tamarack, basswood, walnut, chestnut, and red oak. Her planking and timbers had come out of better wrecks than she. Smith even used railbed ties in her construction. The spar's rigging and canvas came from various dumps and junk piles in the Port Rowan area.

She was narrow, cranky and sluggish. From the day she was launched, she went sideways instead of forward when her sails filled. Why Smith ever built her no one knows. She was too big for fishing, too small for freight, and no one would want her for a pleasure boat, she was so unsightly and unmanageable. She *looked* like a wreck, yet nothing happened to her. Her bow was like an overhanging wedge. She had a flat bottom and a square stern.

In 1898 she was sold for $300 and sailed, sometimes sideways, to Toronto. She was going to be used as a stone-hooker, hauling stone around the lake. This was not at all profitable, as she was too clumsy. Arrangements were made to operate her on a share basis, but this didn't work out.

The *Island Queen* was sold again, and the new owner, thinking he could straighten out her sailing problems and make a profit, decided to enlarge her. This was done, but the ship became more sluggish and unmanageable than ever. Her sails and centreboard were too small — they hadn't got around to enlarging them when they made the vessel bigger. Another party took over, however, and he ended up putting the *Island Queen* on the breakwater in Toronto harbour.

Six more people tried to sail her, but all had the same problems. She was finally abandoned in Frenchman's Bay. There she dragged her anchor and ended up punching a large hole in her bottom. She sank in three feet of water. Her gear was stolen by stone-hooker crews operating in the area.

She was eventually sold for $75. The new owners pried her loose, stuffed an old mattress in the hole in her hull and pumped her out. She was sailed to Port Credit, where she was hauled out. An old elevator was being torn down, so the owner was able to get some old planks and timbers to patch her up. He dropped her keel, and built in a new centreboard box and some deadrise into her bottom. He got an old foremast that had been taken off a schooner. Some old gear and rigging was located, and the ship was ready to go to work. The owner got a contract to transport gravel, but after all the repair work, the ship was still slow and sluggish. However she was a bit more manageable.

She never did much after she was repaired. The owner died several years later and no one claimed her, as she was such a wreck. She was described as having the lines of a flat iron and a Buffalo Creek punt. She was left in Whitby harbour in 1925 and just naturally fell apart, with the assistance of those stealing her timbers for firewood. The last heard of the *Island Queen* was when the Whitby town council insisted the remains of the little schooner be removed, as they were unsightly. So ended the career of the ugly duckling of Long Point, also known as the "Patchwork Hooker."

Idaho, lost off Long Point on November 6, 1897. The most serious marine disaster on the Great Lakes that year.
— *Great Lakes Historical Society*

Idaho

Latitude 42-30-0, longitude 80-07-0. According to *A Guide to Sunken Ships in American Waters* by Lonsdale and Kaplan, that's where the wooden steamer *Idaho* lies. Another report, this from the Simcoe *Reformer*, November 11, 1897, claims the sunken steamer is lying in Long Point Bay, about 12 miles off Port Dover light, with one pole mast sticking out of the water, showing the top peak halyard. A portion of the wreckage was picked up by the fishing tug *German* from Port Dover. In *Lores and Legends*, H. Barrett states that a C.K. Rogers, who was staying at the Ocean House Hotel on Long Point, saw the rescue of two crew members who were clinging to the mast. Barrett also states that the *Idaho* went down off the Cut. Yet another source insists she lies east-southeast of the Old Cut light in 45 feet of water. I have made a thorough search of these areas but to date have not located the *Idaho*. In 1898 her location was known because she was dived on by hardhats who were attempting to salvage her. All they brought up was her compass.

Peck and Masters of Cleveland built the 220-foot propeller boat and launched her in 1863. She carried package freight for the railroad companies. *Idaho* had three distinctive features. Large wooden arches ran along the port and starboard sides of the vessel. They were built into the ship to give the hull strength lengthwise. These were also incorporated into the vessel to keep it from hogging. *Idaho* also had a very different-shaped pilot house. it had eight sides, with ornate woodwork, and at the peak of the roof was a large carved golden eagle. The most outstanding feature was her one and only foremast, approximately 100 feet in height.

With her mast, ornate pilot house, curving arches and her hull painted white, she was a splendid sight to see steaming down the lake, her large flag blowing in the wind, with the name *Idaho* on it in five-foot letters. Her main ports of call were Buffalo, Duluth and Chicago.

After serving many years on the lakes, her age

started to show. Her wooden hull needed constant repair and her boilers and engines were getting to the point where they soon would be beyond fixing. Breakdowns were common. Steel ships were becoming fashionable, as they were safer and not as costly to operate. The *Idaho* was taken out of service and tied up at the dock at Buffalo, where she remained for several seasons. But shipping rates increased substantially during this period, and this encouraged the Western Transportation Company to give her a complete refit and put her back into service.

On Friday morning, November 5, 1897, the *Idaho* left Buffalo under the command of Captain Alexander Gillies. Her cargo consisted of Christmas toys and supplies bound for Milwaukee. En route to her destination she would have to pass Long Point, and this is where she met her demise. Prior to nearing the Point, she encountered a November gale, but the captain decided that the ship was not in danger. They had ploughed through seas of this nature before.

At last the Long Point light was spotted. But, the captain, after discussion with the first mate, decided to continue down the lake and not to seek shelter on the bay side of Long Point.

The trouble began some distance down the lake. *Idaho* started taking on water. It got into the engine room and the fire hold, and the pumps could not keep ahead of it. One of the pumps broke down and a bucket brigade was formed. The water kept coming and put out the fires. The *Idaho* now had no power and she veered in all directions. Battered by the unmerciful waves, some of the crew were washed overboard. Attempts were made to put out the anchors, but in doing so more of the crew were lost. The stern now began to sink and the waves began to roll over the after section of the vessel.

Captain Alexander Gillies was swept overboard by a large wave. He disappeared over the side into the large rollers, never to be seen alive again. Two members of the crew, second mate Louis La Forge and deckhand William Gill, climbed up the tall mast as the ship was going down. They crawled into the crow's-nest, 25 feet above the water. As the *Idaho* settled to the bottom, it took the rest of the crew who were still on deck. La Forge and Gill clung to their position in the mast, and there they stayed, battling cold, rain and hail.

A vessel was sighted at daybreak. They waved frantically, but it did not stop. Around noon the 350-foot steel steamer *Mariposa* spotted them. She was one of the largest ships on the Great Lakes and was captained by Frank Root. She altered course and headed for the two sailors, who were frozen to the mast. A yawl boat was dispatched to rescue the two survivors, but it was smashed by heavy seas. The only alternative was to bring the large *Mariposa* alongside the mast and pluck the sailors off. After three attempts, they were successful, though they had to force the survivors' arms from the mast, as they were covered in ice. Once on board, La Forge and Gill were given comfort and the rescue ship steamed for Buffalo.

At Buffalo Captain Root and members of his crew were given a hero's welcome. Theirs was regarded, and still is, as one of the most amazing feats of navigation and seamanship performed on the Great Lakes. The captain and the crew were all given extra pay for their daring. Captain Root also received a beautiful gold watch.

On November 18, 1897, a notice appeared in the Simcoe *Reformer* which stated that a reward of $50 had been offered for the recovery of the body of Captain Gillies of the *Idaho*. Nearly a year later, in the same newspaper, an article stated that Captain Gillies' body had just washed ashore at Port Maitland.

The old *Idaho*, lost with 19 crew members, was valued at $15,000, her cargo at $100,000. The loss of this vessel was the most serious disaster on the Great Lakes during 1897.

Wooden steamer Niagara lost with all hands on December 5, 1899, off Long Point. — Jim Kidd

Niagara

In December 1899 the following appeared in a Toronto-area newspaper:

LOSS OF THE NIAGARA

It is now certain that the Toronto steamer *Niagara* under Captain Henry McLory foundered last Tuesday evening about eight miles east of Long Point, Lake Erie, with all hands. Numbering sixteen, the names of seven of the crew follows: Captain Henry McLory, Master, Port Colborne; Archie MacDonald, first mate, Bronte; Thomas Mills, first engineer, Toronto; Andrew Leheuch and John I. Morrow, Barrie and Kingston; Annie Morrow, stewardess, Marine City; James Donnelly, Kingston.

The other names of the rest of the crew were not available when this went to press.

The 136-foot wooden steamer had been built at St. Catharines, Ontario, by Melanethon Simpson for the Matthews Line, Toronto, in 1895. The four-year-old *Niagara*, battling 50-mile-an-hour winds and a severe snow storm, came down from Georgian Bay heading for Buffalo. Her cargo consisted of wooden shingles and lumber. Three vessels — *Orion*, *M.T. Green* and the *A.P. Wright* — saw the *Niagara* that Tuesday afternoon. The *A.P. Wright* spotted her a short distance off Long Point. The storm was at its worst off Long Point. Authorities later stated that if *Niagara* had tried to make shelter in the lee of the Point, she would have been battered to pieces before she got there. Wreckage was found about eight miles east of the Point. Included in this was the pilot house, chairs, shingles, lumber and deck beams.

A bottle with a farewell message in it was found washed in at Port Colborne. It read, "Expect to go down any minute. Captain McLory. Good-bye."

When Archie MacDonald, a member of the *Niagara*'s crew was lost, all Bronte was saddened. He was a very popular citizen and played a significant part in community affairs. His body came ashore later that winter in the ice banks near a farm outside Port Maitland. Identification was found on the body, and friends at Bronte were contacted to fetch his remains home. When they arrived, they found that the farmer and his friends had carefully chopped MacDonald out of the ice banks, put him in a box with ice and stored him in the barn. At the funeral service, the undertaker turned the unfortunate sailor's head to one side, as the other side had been ground off by the ice when he came ashore.

Getting an extra trip in before freeze-up is always a risk. Gambling for this extra profit could cost the company a ship and a cargo. This is the chance the *Niagara* took and lost.

Majestic's appearance before she went to the bottom of Lake Erie in 1907. — Institute for Great Lakes Research

Fire on Board — Abandon Ship

Eight miles directly south of Long Point lies the 291-foot wooden propeller steamer *Majestic*. On September 19, 1907, while nearing the base of the Point, fire broke out on the ship. The crew fought the blaze frantically for four hours, trying to get it under control. They poured tons of water throughout the vessel, but this did not stop the consuming blaze.

Realizing the ship was lost and their lives were in danger, boats were lowered and the crew scrambled to safety. *Majestic* burned to the waterline, then sank beneath the waters of Long Point. Very little cargo was lost when she went down, as the ship was travelling light out of Buffalo bound for Toledo.

There was no loss of life, as the crew all got off safely. They were rescued by the propeller steamer *Charlemagne Tower Jr.* and returned to port. All crew members were grateful for being spared from the terror at sea, but were saddened by the loss of their ship.

The engine flywheel, and diver with the video camera. — John Veber

The huge propeller that stopped turning September 19, 1907. — John Veber

Part of the machinery for the steam-powered windless. — John Veber

Because of the severe fire damage, the upper deck machinery fell into the bowels of the vessel. — John Veber

Mike Verbrugge and the author in "Exploration Erie," getting ready for a dive on the Majestic. — Mikoe Visual Productions

Majestic had been built 18 years earlier in the well-known shipyards of James Davidson of West Bay City, Michigan. Her power was a triple expansion engine, with a cylinder and stroke of 20-32x42, made by Fron-tier Works at Detroit. Her scotch boiler was manufactured by M. Riter of Buffalo.

Majestic was located by Mike Verbrugge of Straffordville, who over the years has located and identified a great number of wrecks off Port Burwell and Port Stanley. He is not only a wreck locator and diver, but is also well versed in marine history, ship construction and underwater archaeology. His main concern for the shipwrecks he has located is preservation and conservation. I assisted in the identification of this wreck by supplying research material.

During 1987 Mike Verbrugge and I were asked by Mikoe Visual Productions, Brantford, Ontario, to assist them in making an underwater video of some of the unexplored wrecks in Lake Erie. The purpose of this video, to be called "Exploration Erie," is to show that this area is rich in maritime history and has numerous untouched wrecks. These wrecks are very fragile and must be preserved, as they are rich in maritime history. The request to recreational divers is, "Look and enjoy but do not strip."

Majestic was picked to be one of the wrecks in the video. Lying in 55 feet of water, the *Majestic* makes for a very comfortable dive. Because the ship was burnt to the waterline, the inside of the hull is greatly exposed to view. Her engine and scotch boiler remain reasonably intact. Protruding out of the stern of her hull is the propeller shaft, with the huge propeller completely exposed. It has been idle for 78 years, patiently waiting for steam to be built up in her boiler so she can get under way again.

Scattered on the sandy bottom of the lake are bits of material and gear which at one time were very important in the operation of the vessel. Most people looking at these artifacts today would classify them as junk.

The *Majestic* has now been captured on video for all to see, lying there as intact as she was the day she went to the bottom.

Painting done by the noted Simcoe artist K. Edgar Cantelon of the four girls on the violent waters of Long Point Bay. Each girl was given a copy of this painting by the artist.

The Miracle of Long Point Bay

Tales are told of shipwrecks, bravery and amazing feats of navigation which resulted in survival, but no tale about the Long Point area can top what happened on July 20, 1907.

For eight hours that day, four young ladies — Edna Stickney, 15; Luella Winter, 14; Louise Howick, 15; and her sister Stella Howick, 13 — all from Port Ryerse, amazed all those who lived on the north shore of Lake Erie.

These four young girls were playing in an old row-boat just offshore at Port Ryerse when a northeast wind picked up and the girls realized they were being blown away from shore. None of their families or friends realized the crisis that was unfolding.

The wind picked up and the waters turned from a chop to an almost unmanageable surf. The boat drifted away from shore, and due to the direction the wind was pushing the small, fragile craft, they were headed for the open waters of a very turbulent Lake Erie.

After eight hours of bailing and praying, the wind changed direction and blew them onto the Bluffs. This is one time the notorious sandbar saved lives. Usually a vessel would go aground and be pounded to pieces by the waves, this action not only destroying the vessel but taking lives with it.

At the Bluffs the girls lay down in the sand, exhausted from their misadventure. After a short

This postcard can be found documented in a national book of unique Canadian postcards from the Edwardian era, 1900-1916. The photo for this postcard was taken in the Lynn River, *Simcoe, Ontario, a few days after the girls' rescue. The girls are wearing the same clothes they had on during their 20-mile trip across the bay.*

sleep they were awakened by a barking dog. They followed the animal and it took them to the home of the Secords, who fed the girls and put them to bed.

Earlier in the evening, back at Port Ryerse, the parents had discovered that the girls were missing. To their horror there was no sign of the boat, only stockings and shoes on the beach. Darkness was setting in, the lake had become very rough, and it was impossible to launch a boat. No search could be undertaken until the next morning. The missing girls' families spent a sleepless night thinking of the worst.

At daybreak an intense search was organized by many boats from the area. Their plans were to search the inner and outer bay. All were elated when the girls were found safe and sound at the Bluffs.

How they survived this ordeal was certainly a miracle. If it had not been for the cool-headedness of all four, they would have drowned. Many men under the same circumstances would have lost their heads, upset the boat and been carried away by the rough seas.

The Bluffs, where their fragile boat came to rest and where they were given shelter in the Secords' cabin.
— Dave Stone

What saved the lives of the four girls, according to newspaper accounts at that time, was the courage of Edna Stickney. She was the one who took command and encouraged the others not to lose hope. She kept them bailing the boat to keep it from swamping. She put the boat about with the wind and sat in the stern for eight hours, steering the small craft and, with her back, keeping out the seas that would have sunk it.

The courage of the four girls was praised in local newspapers, and a postcard was made of them, briefly telling of their ordeal. A noted Simcoe artist, K. Edgar Cantelon, even painted a scene of the girls on the boat in the violent waters of Lake Erie. He presented them each with a copy.

The story of this miracle is still being told today.

Pascal P. Pratt, lost on November 16, 1908, off Long Point.
— Great Lakes Historical Society

Pascal P. Pratt

On April 18, 1888, the 272-foot steam propeller *Pascal P. Pratt* was launched at Cleveland. The vessel was built by Thomas Quayle and Sons of Cleveland. Her double compound engine was manufactured by King Iron Works of Buffalo. Originally she had four masts, but these were later removed.

The *Pascal P. Pratt* left Buffalo on November 16, 1908, her destination Milwaukee, with a cargo of anthracite coal. She ran aground on the north side of Long Point. A fire started in the engine room, soon burning the vessel to the waterline. Fortunately her crew escaped the burning ship and eventually found their way to Port Dover. The partially insured vessel was totally destroyed. She sank off Gravelly Bay, Long Point, in 23 feet of water, approximately three miles from the lighthouse. The *Pratt* was owned by Lake Erie Transportation Company at the time of her loss.

In 1909 salvagers removed some of her cargo and machinery. More salvage work was done during the 1960s.

Today the 272 feet of her hull is spread along the sandy bottom. The wreck makes a good dive site, with her bow and stern rising straight up from the bottom. Her great timbers, machinery and boiler are there to explore. She lies in a sandy wasteland, with a scattering of coal near the boiler area. While diving on this wreck I located a horseshoe which was still fastened to a piece of wood. Some sailor had probably brought this on

The stern, with the large propeller shaft protruding from the vessel's hull. — John Veber

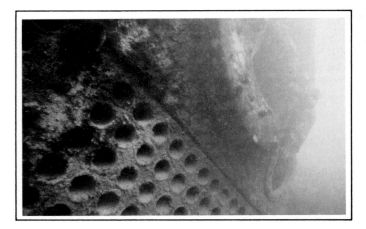

The Pratt's 11½ ft. x 12 ft. scotch boiler, constructed by Lake Erie Boiler Works, Buffalo, N.Y., 1888. — John Veber

The author holding the horseshoe that was on the Pratt for "good luck." — Dave Stone

board and nailed it up for good luck. Examining her bollards, I discovered they were made by the Cleveland Ship Building Company.

Visibility on the wreck runs from 5 to 15 feet. The first dive on the *Pratt* in the spring should be taken with caution. Fish nets could be draped over part of the hull. This also applies to other wrecks in the area. Poor visibility and nets are impending dangers for a diver. Sometimes a fishing net gets its trawl snagged on the wreck and has to leave some of it there to get free. Also, during a bad storm, a gill net can be torn loose from its mooring, drift over the wreck and become tangled in it. The procedure here is to cut the floats off and let the net go to the bottom. If this isn't done, the nets will be fishing forever.

The gravesite of the *Pratt* is alive with schools of bass, rock bass, perch and sunfish. They dart curiously in and out of the wreckage to observe the intruder. Each time, they become bolder and bolder. The *Pascal P. Pratt*, now lying with her skeleton twisted and broken, still serves as a habitat for the creatures of Long Point Bay.

The tug Undertow, with crew on board. — Dave Stone

The Pratt Nearly Had a Bedfellow

During June 1980 the *Pratt* nearly ended up with a companion boat of much smaller size. What boat was this? Mine, the 22-foot *Beachcomber*.

On board was the author, Mike Fletcher, a well-known wreck diver with many finds to his credit, and a friend of his from Brantford. We were on the wreck site of the *Pratt*, along with the Port Dover tug *Undertow*, owned by Dave Matthews of Port Dover. The day had been planned for diving, but it didn't work out to our satisfaction.

On the trip out to the end of the Point, the weather had been favourable and forecasts predicted it would stay this way. How wrong they were! A very black sky, almost nightlike, was moving towards us from the

northeast. The water was changing from a calm to ripples and then waves. We knew we were going to get caught in a fierce summer squall.

Darkness set in around us, with gale-force winds and driving rains. It was too late to put the boat top up; we were soaking wet and the waters had become so violent we couldn't manage this task if we tried. We signalled the *Undertow* to head for Dover, not wanting it to get caught on the Bluff Bar. It started on its way, momentarily visible and then it was gone behind the rollers.

The lake had become so rough I realized there was no way I would survive by going around the outer buoy at the end of the Bluff Bar. My only alternative was to try and cross the bar at the Bluffs. As we neared the bar, I could see by the wave action that sometimes the bar was completely exposed. The idea was to run aground on the bar and leave the boat. At this point, who cared about property. It was our lives that we were concerned with. We planned to walk the bar ashore to safety.

Again we got a surprise, large combers pushed the boat onto the bar, then another wave hit us and moved the boat closer to shore. This happened again and again. The next thing we noticed, we were floating free, being moved by the driving wind and rain through an opening into the marsh. We knew we were going to end up in shallow water, deep in the muck at the far end.

Two anchors were thrown out with plenty of rope, but to no avail; the anchors would not hold in the muck. With the engine not running, nothing was going to stop us.

In the marsh was an old dredge. My friend Mike Fletcher grabbed a line to see if he could lasso it. With only one opportunity to do this, as we were moving so fast, it had to be a good throw. He did it, we tied up and we were in safe harbour.

We put the top up, got the bilge pump working, and stayed there till it settled down. It became calm, the sun came out, and it was hard to believe anything had happened.

The *Undertow* made it back to Port Dover after hours of battling high seas. The *Beachcomber* survived this ordeal, as well. Who says aluminum boats aren't tough. This Starcraft took all that punishment and has taken much more since.

The Pascal P. Pratt didn't get a bedfellow and remains there quietly undisturbed! Dave Stone and Mike Fletcher at the wreck site of the Pascal P. Pratt. — Mark Ansley

Marquette & Bessemer #2 went to the bottom in 1909, taking 33 lives.

Marquette & Bessemer #2

One of the mysteries of Lake Erie is the tragic sinking of the 350-foot car ferry *Marquette & Bessemer #2*. She sank with 33 crew members and one passenger. Some authorities think she was lost mid-length off Long Point, others think off Port Stanley, Port Burwell or in the middle of the lake. The following is why she could be on the bottom at one of these locations.

She left Conneaut, Ohio, in a gale on December 9, 1909, with a cargo of 26 train cars of coal, 3 cars containing steel and 1 with iron castings. Also on board was a passenger, who brought on $50,000 in cash for a deal he had made in Ontario. The *Marquette & Bessemer #2* was bound for Port Stanley, her regular run. The moment she steamed out of Conneaut harbour was the moment she joined "The Ghost Fleet," never to be seen or heard from again.

When the *Marquette & Bessemer #2* was built in 1905 by the American Ship Building Company of Cleve-

land for her new owners, Marquette & Bessemer Dock and Navigation Company, it was decided the vessel did not need a stern gate. The function of the gate, when put into position once the ship was loaded, was to protect the ship against seas coming over the stern and going down the hatches to flood the hold. The company felt it was just an extra expense, and that if the ship got into bad weather, all she had to do was head the vessel into the rough seas.

Old-timers had thoughts on what happened to the ship. She could have made it to Port Stanley but found that the weather was so bad she couldn't enter the harbour. She might then have headed west to Rondeau, battling one of the worst gales in years, only to find she couldn't make it into Rondeau harbour either. The ship might then have headed back to Port Stanley, then to Conneaut, unable to touch land at either. Finally, in desperation, she perhaps headed for Long

A funeral service conducted by Shelley B. Cook, lighthouse keeper, at Long Point lighthouse for William Wilson, wheelsman of the Marquette & Bessemer #2. His body washed ashore a year after the sinking of the car ferry. He was identified by the serial number on his gold watch. — Mrs. Lorne Brown

Crude wooden headboard marking William Wilson's grave near the second lighthouse. High water eventually washed the headboard out, then the grave, and finally Wilson's body, returning it to the sea. — Mrs. Lorne Brown

Point to seek shelter behind its long arm. Reports at the time also stated that it was believed the violent waters came over the stern, poured through the hatches, flooded the hold, and down she went.

The four lifeboats were located: one with nine frozen bodies in it off Erie; two off Port Burwell, one empty but sound, the other smashed; and the last broken in two and smashed into the seawall at Buffalo. A lot of debris from the ship washed ashore between Port Burwell and the tip of Long Point. The body of Captain Robert McLeod was found ten months later on Long Point. About a year after the sinking, William Wilson's body came ashore near the tip of Long Point.

He was buried on the Point by Shelley Cook, the lighthouse keeper. A wooden headboard was erected over his grave. Years later high water washed out the headboard, then the grave, and then the remains of the wheelsman from the *Marquette & Bessemer #2*.

The day the car ferry battled Lake Erie, there were 30 ships anchored on the lee side of the Point, riding out the storm.

The *Marquette & Bessemer #2* has yet to be found, but she will be some day. Somewhere she lies nobly, her steel hull a shroud for those unfortunate souls who were trapped inside at the time of the sinking.

Steamer Elphicke, lost on Long Point,
October 19, 1913.
— W.A. Gordon

Elphicke

The 273-foot wooden propeller steamer *Elphicke* left Fort William with a cargo of 106,000 bushels of grain. She was bound for Buffalo. Captain A.B. Cummings and his crew of 17 were hoping for good weather on this long trip. The 24-year-old vessel had been built by the Craig Ship Building Company of Trenton, Michigan. She was launched on July 3, 1889. At the launching her gross tonnage was 2,058 tons. Later on she was rebuilt, and at the time of her sinking her gross tonnage was 2,406 tons. Her triple expansion engine was built by S.F. Hodge and Company of Detroit, Michigan, and the 11½ by 11 foot boiler was supplied by F.M. McGregor, Detroit.

Elphicke travelled down the upper lakes from Fort Williams in fair weather, and there were no unusual occurrences. However, in the Detroit River, her fortune changed. The ship bottomed out on a shoal of some nature. The hull was assessed for damage, but there was nothing visible.

The wooden steamer made her way into Lake Erie, still in good weather conditions. Some distance from Long Point, conditions changed dramatically to a full-blown gale. *Elphicke* began to leak in the weather. The pumps were started but could not keep ahead of the water flooding the hold. Once again the hull was checked, and this time a large hole was discovered.

The ship was now taking a severe beating from the violent waves, and her seams started to open up. The pumps were going to full capacity, but the water level in the hull continued to rise. It became apparent that the ship was going to sink. Captain Cummings decided to beach her. That way the crew would be out of danger and the *Elphicke* could be salvaged.

She ran aground approximately 600 yards from shore on October 19, 1913. The crew put out a boat, but the angry waters demolished it. The men tossed out of the boat were able to get back on board the stranded ship. The Long Point lifesaving station crew

The rough seas had broken the Elphicke's back by the time the underwriters arrived. She was a total loss. — W.A. Gordon

Hawsepipe from the Elphicke recovered by Lorne Brown, lighthouse keeper 1928-1955. — Dave Stone

quickly arrived on the scene. Their surf boat reached the anxious sailors and brought them safely to shore.

The captain informed the owners, the Buckeye Steamship Company of Cleveland, of their loss. The owners notified the underwriters to come and inspect the *Elphicke*. By the time they arrived the vessel had broken her back. She was a total loss, and the cargo was a complete write off. At the hearing concerning the loss of the *Elphicke*, the Steamship Inspection Service found no fault against those in command.

Today bits and pieces of the *Elphicke* still lie on the sandy bottom on the south shore, just west of the lighthouse, in a depth of 16 feet of water. *Elphicke* acts like a snow fence, gathering sand from the currents flowing through her remains, covering them up. The ship's timbers stay covered until a south gale washes away the sand. After a big storm, if one is observant, pieces of the *Elphicke* can be seen on the beach.

An October Mourning

When Friday, October 16, 1916, was over, people were shocked at the loss of men and ships that had occurred during those 24 hours. The day became known locally as "Black Friday." I could finally understand the terror of the situation when I met an old sailor who had lived through it.

Many years ago I was staying overnight in the village of Tobermory, Ontario. I made arrangements to board the ferry for Manitoulin Island the next day. Having some hours to kill, I headed for the docks. After checking out the dive boats, I noticed an elderly, weather-beaten man sitting there fishing. He looked like an "old salt," so I thought talking to him would be an interesting way to pass the time.

After we talked briefly about fishing, he told me he had spent most of his life sailing the Great Lakes. Being an old sailor myself, we could easily identify with each other, even though his time had been spent on fresh water and mine on salt.

He informed me that as a very young man he had gone to work as a coal passer on an old steamer. That day was Friday, October 16, 1916.

The vessel he was on had been bucking high seas most of the day. Down in the stokehold, he didn't realize what was going on. He knew that if he didn't hang on to something, he'd be flat on the deck again, having gone through this routine the past three hours of being tossed around. He was terrified listening to the crashing and pounding, but the real crunch came when the ship had a hatch cover torn off and the lake came pouring in.

He just knew the ship wasn't going to make it. He decided right then to go and see the captain, a seasoned veteran. If he could talk to the captain, he was sure he would regain his confidence and have no reason to be so fearful.

An old sailor telling his story about "Black Friday" to the author. — Dave Stone

With great difficulty he managed to reach the captain's cabin. Finding the door shut, he knocked loudly and waited a minute. There was no response. He repeated this several times with no results. Finally, in desperation, he turned the knob and pushed the door open. Suddenly the confidence he was starting to rebuild disappeared. There was the captain, down on his knees praying.

He returned to the stokehold still full of fear. Little did he realize the destruction of lives and ships taking place.

What has "Black Friday" got to do with Long Point? Two ships, the *Meridia* and the *James B. Colgate*, both familiar sights in Long Point waters during their lengthy careers, were lost that day.

The *James B. Colgate*, leaving Buffalo with a cargo of coal, encountered terrible seas off Long Point. Caught in the roughest part of Lake Erie, she was having trouble with the ten-foot waves. She worked her way up the

James B. Colgate, the whaleback steamer lost on October 16, 1916. There was one survivor. This vessel has not yet been located by divers. — Great Lakes Historical Society

Merida, the bulk freighter lost on October 16, 1916, with her crew of 23. — Great Lakes Historical Society

lake in a gale, battling seas that gave her no mercy. The ship was taking on water faster than the pumps could handle it. Finally, after struggling against the fury of the lake all day, the *Colgate* slid to the bottom with her crew of 26. The only survivor was Captain Walter Grashaw. He was floating in the lake in the darkness, trying to keep his head above water, when he bumped into a raft. He climbed on and clung to it for 35 hours. He was finally picked up more dead than alive by the second *Marquette & Bessemer*. He lived to tell the story of what happened to his ship on "Black Friday."

The 308-foot *Colgate* was built by the American Steel Barge Company at Superior, Wisconsin, in 1892. She was powered by a triple expansion steam engine built by the Marinette Iron Works of Duluth, Minnesota. Her 12 by 13 foot scotch boiler was built in 1892 by Milwaukee Boiler Works. When she sank, her owners were the Standard Transit Company of Minnesota.

The *James B. Colgate* was the first whaleback steamer to be lost on the Great Lakes. Her final resting place is not yet known. However, some maritime historians estimate that she lies somewhere 20 miles southwest of Long Point.

The other vessel, *Merida*, a Canadian steel-hulled bulk freighter, was thought to be on a course from Southeast Shoal to Long Point when she went down with the crew of 23 on board. She had sailed from Fort William bound for Buffalo with a cargo of iron and was last seen by the steamer *Briton* near Southeast Shoal. The captain of the *Briton* stated that it was one of the worst storms he had ever seen on Lake Erie. He witnessed the *Merida* taking heavy weather, but thought she seemed to be handling it.

The ore carrier could not take the beating the lake was rendering. She plunged to the bottom with all hands. The bodies of the crew and debris were found by commercial fishermen out of Port Stanley. The wreck was found a number of years later by Larry Jackson of Port Stanley. David Knowles and Roy Everett

The bilge pump that couldn't keep ahead of the mountainous waves that sent the Merida to the bottom. — John Veber

Merida's ghostly hull spelling out her name. — John Veber

dove on the wreck and found it sitting upright and in good condition. She rests in approximately 75 feet of water south and west of Port Stanley.

When the disaster occurred, the 378-foot vessel was owned by the Valley Camp Company. She was built in 1893 by the F.W. Wheeler Company in West Bay City, Michigan. The *Merida* was at one time classed as the largest ship on the Great Lakes.

During the storm, with the 75-mile-an-hour winds, two other ships were also lost in Lake Erie, making it a total of four ships and 51 lives lost.

Never again were the *Merida* or the *James B. Colgate* seen off Long Point, plying up or down the lake to distant ports.

Ballords on the deck with chain still in place. — John Veber

Lawrence as she looked before being converted to a steam barge.
— *Great Lakes Historical Society*

Lawrence

The 135-foot wooden propeller steamer *Lawrence* was built at Cleveland in 1868. Her original owners were the Northern Transportation Company. She was to be used for the freight and passenger trade from Chicago to Ogdensburg. She was trim-looking vessel with an all-white hull, cabins trimmed in green and the stacks black with white tops. She was rigged for a fore and aft sail, and the tall mast was forward. Steamers in the passenger trade during this time were required to carry sail in case of emergency.

Lawrence stayed in the ownership of the North Transportation Company until the early 1880s, when the company went out of business. She was then sold to the Northern Michigan Transportation Company of Chicago. This company merged with Seymour Lines in 1895. The vessel was sold, but she continued to operate, carrying passengers and fruit between lower Lake Michigan ports and Chicago. During 1900 she was rebuilt and lengthened 34 feet. At this time her name was changed to *Frontenac*. Ten years later the ship was converted to a steam barge and renamed *H.N. Jex*. With this conversion she became a coal carrier from Detroit to Lake Erie ports. The barge was then sold to a Canadian shipping company in 1915 and continued to carry coarse freight.

On August 16, 1921, she was caught in a fierce summer storm off Long Point. The vessel could not take the violent pounding of the lake and floundered. She had been in service in one form of vessel or another for 53 years.

*City of Dresden, "The Whisky Ship,"
lost November 18, 1922.
— Great Lakes Historical Society*

Free Whisky — No Prescription Required

The wooden propeller steamer *City of Dresden* was built by Jenkins Shipbuilding Company and launched at Walkerville, Ontario, in 1872. She was put into service to run between Detroit, Dresden and Wallaceburg. Travellers who preferred a leisurely trip could take this new upper-cabin steamer, which left Dresden every Tuesday, Thursday and Saturday, with the return trip on alternate days. Captain J. Weston was in charge during the early years. In 1886 the vessel's run became Windsor to Leamington.

She was rebuilt in 1888 and sailed from Sandusky, Ohio, to Canadian ports. During 1892 John Doty Engine Company of Toronto built a fore and aft compound engine for her with a cylinder and stroke of 15-26x18. Then, during 1906, Park Brothers of Chatham, Ontario, installed a 6 foot by 12 foot firebox boiler. The vessel was purchased by Captain Sylvester

McQueen of Amherstburg, Ontario, in 1914. At the time McQueen purchased the steamer, she was 42 years old, showing her age and rapidly approaching the stage where she would be unseaworthy and irreparable. However she was patched up and her life was extended another eight years.

On November 17, 1922, the *City of Dresden* left the dock at Belleville with a cargo of Corby's Special Selected and Old Crow. The value on the manifest was $65,000. The cargo was stowed, with bottles below decks and cases and barrels above deck. Her official papers stated that this cargo was going to Mexico. How could a ship like the *City of Dresden* make it to Mexico? Well, it had no intention of going there. This was just a way of getting around the existing laws. As long as a ship didn't have an official destination in the United States or Canada, the large cargo of liquor was legal. A ship could leave a Canadian port with clearance papers from customs, destination Jamaica, and be back empty in a few hours take on another cargo to Cuba. The real ports of call were in Ontario or the United States, or perhaps the ship would meet another vessel and transfer the cargo aboard it.

Ontario had some strange laws regarding spirits. Under the Ontario Temperance Act, we could make and export whisky but not drink it. The only way one could acquire a bottle was to have a prescription from the doctor. It was to be taken for health reasons only. The friendly local druggist would dispense the whisky for you, then the two of you would end up in the back room of the drugstore. You would leave empty-handed, but your health would be greatly improved. As for the druggist, he had made a sale and had also had the privilege of drinking part of it.

Bootlegging was a booming business, and ships like the *City of Dresden* were all getting a piece of the action. This was the business the steamer was engaged in on Friday, November 17, 1922. She steamed into the Bay of Quinte, up Lake Ontario to the Welland Canal, with little consequence. However, upon entering Lake Erie, conditions changed drastically. The winds from the north were creating huge waves. The *City of Dresden*, being old and underpowered, was running into difficulty. The captain decided to throw her anchors out and ride out the storm in the Gravelly Bay area. The winds became stronger and she started to drag her anchors. They decided to move around to the south shore. But the underpowered vessel could not handle the rough seas, so off came the deck cargo, 42 cases of whisky, to lighten the vessel. While this helped the situation considerably, allowing her to round the Point, it was only a temporary relief, because the winds shifted to the southwest. Blinded by the high seas and being badly pounded by gale-force winds, the *City of Dresden* just barely made her way down the shore. The seams started to let go and flooding began in the hold. The captain decided to beach her at the cove. He was reluctant to do so with the remaining cargo he had on board, but he had no other choice. She grounded on a bar about 300 yards from shore. Immediately she started to break up. It was now 4:30 p.m., November 18.

Before hitting the bar, the captain blew the whistle repeatedly to let those nearby know that his ship was in distress. Two lifeboats were launched. The crew scrambled aboard but, to their horror, both boats overturned. The captain's son, Peregrime, was washed away by the raging surf and was never seen alive again. One lifeboat was righted and the crew got in, but they had no oars. The lifeboat wallowed aimlessly in the foaming water.

Not far from the cove where the *Dresden* became stranded was the Delbert Rockefeller farm. Pearl Rockefeller, Viola Blackenbury and Mrs. Rockefeller's mother had heard the distress whistle, immediately hooked up the horse and buggy, and headed for the beach at breakneck speed. When they spotted the wallowing lifeboat, the two younger women waded into the raging breakers, caught a line from the lifeboat and pulled it ashore.

Meanwhile others in the area heard the distress whistle and headed for the beach. They couldn't believe their eyes — bottles and more bottles were floating ashore. They swam out to get the whisky, ignoring Pearl Rockefeller and her niece struggling with half-drowned crew. The scavengers would swim out to where the bottles were floating, bring them ashore, bury them in the sand and go back for more. As fast as someone buried a bottle in the sand, someone else would dig it up, drink it or bury it elsewhere. The beach area now began to look like a three-ring circus. Everything that moved on wheels was on the beach — cars, buggies, wagons, bicycles, wheelbarrows and even baby buggies — all being loaded up with Old Crow or Corby's Special Selected. The scavengers showed no preference.

The crew of the *City of Dresden* were taken to the

Action on the beach late Saturday afternoon. — *Julia Stone*

They hid it in the pig pens. — *Julia Stone*

Rockefeller home for comfort and shelter.

At Gravelly Bay, one of the crew of the lifesaving station spotted something floating ashore. He was overwhelmed when he discovered it to be a case of whisky. The he saw another and another. Eventually he ended up with 42 cases. He didn't tell any other members of the crew about his find. He buried each case beside one of the 42 telephone poles which serviced the lighthouse. Nothing was done about his find until months later, when things had settled back to normal. He then sold his cache to a bootlegger and paid off the mortgage on his house.

Back on the beach, the whole community was present. Some were drinking, some were drunk, others were carting it away. Some hid their find from the police, who would soon be on their trail. They tied the bottles in sacks and hid them in the marsh or creeks in the outhouses, down the wells, in the pig pens. One farmer lined the eavestroughs of his barn and prayed it wouldn't rain. Another ploughed a furrow in his field and then turned the furrow back over, burying his

loot. So that the authorities wouldn't question why he had ploughed the line strip down his field, he put up a fence all along the ploughed area. A good place to hide the bottles was in the false ceilings of their homes. One enterprising young man tied the bottles along his rail fences, and the long grass hid them from sight. People, because of their great haste or due to the influence of whisky, had a great deal of difficulty the next day remembering where they had stashed their loot. One of the smartest moves was made by an individual who cut the telephone lines to Simcoe. The authorities were not notified of the theft of all this whisky until after everyone had it hidden.

Ben Harris, who was my favourite Long Point person, told me the following story. He was in on the action the day the *City of Dresden* was wrecked. At that time he was working in a mill on the outskirts of Port Rowan. He, like most, went down to the beach when the distress whistle was heard. Lo and behold, there was all this booze on the beach. Without hesitation he gathered up a large number of bottles, took them back

And down the wells. — Julia Stone

Someone cut the telephone lines to Simcoe. — Julia Stone

to the mill and hid them in various places. He placed dusty feedbags over them and had the place looking as if nothing had been disturbed. Several days later he received a visitor, police inspector "Dickey" Edmonds. Inspector Edmonds asked Ben if he had any whisky, and Ben's reply was "certainly not." The police then searched the mill and came up with nothing. Ben said he sweated blood because he was sure they would look under some of those dusty bags covering the bottles. after the search, Inspector Edmonds turned to Ben and thanked him for being so honest. He said, "I wish there were more Christian boys like you in Port Rowan."

Ben and his cousin also hid several kegs in the marsh. After things cooled off they went back to find and sample their wares. But the only way they could locate the kegs in the marsh was with the use of a sharp-pointed spud. They would poke this thing into the ooze until they hit something hard. If they punched a hole in one of the kegs and some swamp water seeped in, that didn't matter. The free whisky still tasted pretty good.

Doc Roher of Port Rowan told me he was a very young lad at the time of the shipwreck. He said that one day he and his father had gone to Port Rowan late in the afternoon with the horse and buggy. On the way home they too heard the steamer's whistle, and half the population of Port Rowan went by them as if there was no tomorrow. The Rohers lived at Erieview, not far from the Delbert Rockefeller farm, where the sound seemed to be coming from. They went home and Doc's father put him to bed. He couldn't understand this, as it was still light. His father also went to bed. When he got up the next morning, he found his father sitting on the edge of the bed, holding his head and very, very sick. His father had slipped out as soon as his son had fallen asleep and joined the big booze bash.

When the investigation was completed by the police and other authorities who had searched the beaches, buildings and the surrounding area, no evidence had been found of the *City of Dresden*'s cargo. Most of the population were questioned and nobody knew anything about it. The police tried to prosecute some of these outstanding citizens, but nothing would stand up in court, as there were no witnesses.

For years, the bottles and kegs continued to show up. They would be washed ashore or be found where someone had hidden them and forgotten. Hogs rooted up bottles around the farmyards. One farmer found three cases while putting a new tile in his ditch. A fireman, fighting a fire in Port Rowan, put his axe through a false ceiling and down came some Old Crow. An old house was being torn down in the village, and as the plaster was being knocked off, they found five bottles tucked along the studding, aging nicely.

The *City of Dresden* was completely broken up except for part of the deckhouse, which was washed ashore. Her remains were scattered along the beach, accompanied by hundreds of empty bottles. One lifeboat mysteriously disappeared into a nearby farmer's barn. The next year the engine was salvaged by Captain McQueen and Ray Sawyer, the ship's engineer. The body of Peregrime McQueen, the captain's son, was washed ashore shortly after the wreck.

What a glorious time the Port Rowan-area folk had with the 8,000 gallons of corn and rye whisky. Long Point has never been the same since. One can be sure some of this loot is still hidden from view. It's just waiting to be found, for glasses to be filled and toasts to be made to the whisky ship, *City of Dresden*.

The tug Angler.

Angler

The tug *Angler*, a work boat used to transport people and supplies in the Long Point area. It would often ply out of Port Ryerse, St. Williams and Port Rowan. During 1925 *Angler* caught fire and sank between the Rice Bay Club and the Long Point Company cottages. Most sport fishermen, still getting their fishing lures snagged on the remains of the hull, are unaware of its existence.

Aycliffe Hall

The 253-foot *Aycliffe Hall* collided with the United States steamer *Edward J. Berwind* approximately 16 miles off the end of Long Point on June 11, 1936, while travelling through a dense fog. Her destination was Collingwood, and she was running light when she left Sorel, Quebec. *Aycliffe Hall* was a British-built propeller launched in 1928 by Smith's Dock Company, South Bank-on-Tees, Great Britain. Her triple expansion engine, with cylinder and stroke of 15-25-40 x 33 was also built by Smith's. Blair and Company Limited of Stockton-on-Tees built the 10 foot 6 inch by 11 foot scotch boiler. The *Aycliffe Hall* was owned by the Hall Transportation Company of Canada when she was lost.

Fortunately, at the time of the collision, there was no loss of life. The vessel had been cut beside the boiler, and she sat with her spar half out of the water and creating a menace to navigation in the channel. Tom Reid Salvage Company of Sarnia accepted the challenge of removing this hazard. (This salvage company was the most enterprising one of this period, under the capable management of Captain Tim Reid.) With an air compressor, the bow was floated so it was out of the water. Plans had been made to raise the ship, but the hole in her side was too big to patch. The midship bulkhead was strengthened and four pontoons were put under her stern. The divers went down to blow out the water in the pontoons and discovered they had disappeared. They had broken loose, even with the chains fastened around them.

The Reid Company decided to drag the ship into shallow water, but a storm came up and she rolled over. She slid into a deep hole in the bottom of Lake Erie.

The canaller *Aycliffe Hall* remained on the bottom of Lake Erie, with the Dominion government greatly concerned about the danger it posed to navigation, although there is little doubt that the superstructure of the ship was scraped down by the lake ice in succeeding winters. On July 18, 1939, the hull was located in 12 fathoms of water by divers from the United States Coast Guard. The Canadian Department of Transport buoy-tender *Grenville* attended the scene and used explosives to level the wreck so it would not interfere with passing ships. This ended the possibility of the ship ever being raised, either for reconstruction or scrapping.

The remains of the *Aycliffe Hall* lie in the Graveyard of the Great Lakes. A ship was lost, but the crew lived to sail another day.

James H. Reed, "Grand Old Lady of the Lakes," lost in Lake Erie on April 27, 1944, taking with her ten of her crew.

Death in the Fog

The Long Point light casts its comforting beams 30 miles out into the lake as it makes a revolution on its turntable. It sends out a soft blanket of light that travels over the graves of sunken ships. But the resting place of the *James H. Reed* lies out of reach, approximately 37 miles southwest of Long Point. Her remains lie in 70 feet of water, scattered in a thousand pieces the length of her 448-foot hull.

Built during 1903 by the Detroit Ship Building Company at Wyandotte, Michigan, this ore carrier was a giant in her time. She plied the lakes for 39 years, until fog put an end to her career. Like many of the lakers during this period, she had no radar to combat the silent killer fog.

On April 27, 1944, the doomed vessel left Escabana, Michigan, bound for Buffalo with a cargo of iron ore for the war effort. During wartime the lakes were busier than usual. Cargoes such as iron ore, to be used in the manufacture of tools of war, moved hurriedly up and down the lakes. These necessary supplies were always wanted yesterday.

On that fateful day, the ship, travelling in a heavy fog, collided with the coal carrier *Ashcroft*. As a result of the collision, the *Reed* was laid open. The lake rushed in and ten crew members went to their deaths. The *Ashcroft*, damaged but still afloat, picked up the remaining members of the crew. These 24 survivors were taken to Ashtabula.

The location of the *James H. Reed's* grave created a problem. Lying in the shipping lanes, with her masts protruding from the water, she was a navigational hazard. To overcome this dangerous situation her hull was blown up by the U.S. Army Corps of Engineers. Not only was the superstructure cleared off, but the hull was completely flattened. When diving on this wreck, it takes a bit of time to get oriented because of the complete destruction of the vessel.

What did the crew on board the *James H. Reed* feel while travelling through that dense fog? I know, because I experienced exactly the same situation, only it was in the North Atlantic, two days out of St. Johns, Newfoundland. By coincidence, it was in April 1944!

I was a crew member on board the corvette H.M.C.S. *Chilliwack*, escorting a convoy of 62 merchant ships from Londonderry, Ireland, to St. Johns, Newfoundland. As we approached our destination we encountered fog that you could cut with a knife. To make matters worse, our radar was down, and we ended up out of position and on the inside of the convoy. It was evident we were going to collide with a merchantman.

With whistles blasting to warn of nearby ships, we groped through the fog. To our horror, we could see the faint outline of a large grey hull crossing our bow. Worse still, immediately off our starboard side appeared another ship, so close you could touch it. Terrified, we waited for the impact of collision. In fact we were so sure this was going to happen that we went to collision stations.

Through Lady Luck, all vessels survived the close call and made it to their destinations without a scratch. Death took a holiday that day for the crew of the *Chilliwack* on the North Atlantic, but not for some crew members of the *James H. Reed* on Lake Erie.

One of the old wooden fishing tugs, Brown Brothers, was lost off Long Point in 1959.

Brown Brothers

The 75-foot wooden fish tug was built in Port Stanley by Thomas Thurstin. She spent most of her 44 years fishing in Long Point and area waters.

In 1946 she was sold to Thomas Ivey and Sons, and for the next four years she was called the *Iveyrose*. In 1950 she was converted to diesel. That same year the tug was sold and her name was changed again, back to *Brown Brothers*.

The old vessel was sunk in a violent storm approximately four and a half miles north-northeast of Long Point. No lives were lost when she went down on October 28, 1959.

94

The sloop Gus when she first went aground on Pottahawk Bar. — Dave Stone

The Gus, three weeks later, battered to pieces by the destructive wave action. — Dave Stone.

Gus

On September 2, 1972, the 46-foot sloop *Gus* had just completed a major refit at the Erie Yacht Club, Pennsylvania. On this day she sailed on her maiden voyage after refit, from Erie to Long Point. En route she sprang a leak and began taking on water faster than her pumps could handle it. The owner, Robert Heinrich, reportedly ran her aground on a sandbar off Pottahawk Point, Long Point, to keep the vessel from sinking. (Pottahawk is located approximately eight kilometres south of Turkey Point.) The crew of two on board made it to shore safely,

The *Gus* split her hull when she grounded on the sandbar and seemed doomed as she lay on her side, her deck awash and the waves pounding on her hull, threatening to break her up. If she wasn't salvaged immediately, the first big storm would render her a total loss.

But there was no attempt made to save the *Gus* from her plight. The owner tried to locate someone to salvage the sloop but to no avail. In the meantime looters began stripping from the hull any valuables that could be removed. Both the R.C.M.P. and the customs officials were notified, but this still didn't stop the pillage. Time was running out. Aground on a sandbar is no place to be on Long Point Bay. Because it is so shallow, it just takes a brisk wind to start up a violent sea with pounding waves that will destroy anything in their way.

This happened, and in less than three weeks she was broken up completely. Part of her hull was torn loose from the clutching sandbar, carried east of the bar and deposited in a weed bed, where it lies today. Other bits and pieces were eventually washed up on the beaches of Ryerson and Second islands.

Aletha B.

Early on the morning of Sunday, March 24, 1974, nine fishing tugs left their berths in Port Dover harbour in fine weather. Fishing had been good most of the winter and recently there had been a good run of smelt. On board the 56-foot trawler *Aletha B.* was Captain Allan Perry, who had been fishing with the *Aletha B.* less than a year, and his brother Wayne.

In the early afternoon the westerly winds picked up considerably in the outer Long Point Bay area where they were trawling. In the stormy waters nearby was the *Trimac*, also trawling. Shortly before three o'clock Captain Terry Hagen of *Trimac* radioed the *Aletha B.* and was informed that everything was fine. *Trimac* moved away from the tug, assured that all was well. However, five minutes later, they received a call from the *Aletha B.* saying she was in trouble. *Trimac* headed back to the distressed vessel and found it upside down, with no trace of the crew. Ten- to 12-foot waves had capsized the fishing tug.

Captain Hagen and his crewman, Jim Lindsay, threw out a float where the stricken vessel sank and proceeded to search the area desperately for the two crew members. The poor water conditions made it very difficult, and soon *Trimac* was also having trouble. Finally they had to give up and head into port.

Later that same afternoon a U.S. Coast Guard helicopter started searching and was joined by a search plane from the Canadian Forces base at Trenton. Both aircraft searched until darkness set in. The next day the search continued, and finally a tug located the *Aletha B.* with a depth sounder. The tug was lying in 90 feet of water. It was still too rough to put divers down and search for the crew. Eventually the vessel was brought to the surface by the use of a crane and brought back to her home port of Port Dover. No trace of the crew was found in the vicinity.

After a refit the *Aletha B.* rejoined the fishing fleet and sailed out again to challenge the Long Point waters.

The community of Port Dover will never forget the loss of two of their finest young fishermen.

The Stanley Clipper as she appeared shortly after being brought home to Port Dover.
—Dave Stone

Stanley Clipper

The *Stanley Clipper*, a 62-foot fishing tug, was built at Port Colborne in 1938 and rebuilt in 1960. Over the years she had been engaged in commercial fishing in Lake Erie and owned by Misner Fisheries Limited of Port Dover. She was valued at $150,000.

She left Port Dover harbour in the early morning hours of April 30, 1984, with her sister fishing tug *Ciscoette*. On board were Captain James Saunders and crew members John Mummery and Daryl Clement, all of Port Dover. These well-respected men were experienced fishermen and all came from long-time fishing families. They were all very knowledgeable in the ways of Lake Erie.

When the fishing tugs left early that morning, there was only a slight swell, but around 11 a.m. the winds started to blow up. They had been fishing for smelt around the tip of Long Point, well down the south shore. Both tugs had taken a good catch and were headed home. Travelling east, they rounded the end of the Point and found the seas building up so badly they had to head into the west to break the 12- to 15-foot seas. The speed was checked down to try and handle the violent lake.

The *Ciscoette* was approximately a half a mile behind the *Stanley Clipper* and eventually lost visual contact, but remained in touch by radio and radar. Winds over 70 miles per hour were reported around 2 p.m. The *Stanley Clipper*'s crew members made contact with the shore, saying they were in trouble. Then a Mayday was heard by an Ontario Provincial Police patrol boat and

Stanley Clipper raised with air bags, but not high enough to have her pumped out. In the background is the Ciscoette. — Dave Stone

Diver on board attempting to adjust the airbags. — Dave Stone

another fishing tug. Still in radio contact, the *Ciscoette* heard the *Stanley Clipper*'s final message: "We're going over. Oh my God, what a way to go." Then the *Ciscoette* lost radio and radar contact. A large wave had broken over the *Ciscoette*'s bow, smashing the wheelhouse window and putting the radar out of order.

Ciscoette searched for the *Stanley Clipper* and her crew until darkness set in. Other fishing tugs and air rescue crews began to search. The tugs battled gale-force winds and savage waves which threatened them with the same fate as the missing vessel. Some debris and lifejackets were located in Long Point Bay and were identified as being from the lost fishing tug. It was hoped that perhaps the crew members had made it to shore somewhere on Long Point, but it was also realized that no one could survive for long in the bitterly cold waters reported at 7°C.

The next day the search was on again, using aircraft and many fishing tugs, but the boats were hampered by the high winds and massive waves, and the search had to be called off for those on the water.

On the third day the *Stanley Clipper* was located by a fishing tug approximately three and a half miles east of Ryerson Island. Estimates were that she was in about 38 feet of water. The vessel was found sitting upright and was identified by Ontario Provincial Police divers. The sunken boat was searched thoroughly, but they found no members of the crew on board or in the immediate area. Poor visibility hampered the efforts of divers. The search for the missing crew was continued for a number of days by divers and aircraft, with no success, and eventually the search was called off.

A memorial service was held for the three missing men, at Grace United Church, Port Dover. Their loss was a tremendous shock to the whole community. The attendance of over 800 at this service showed the respect the people of Port Dover had for the lost crew and their bereaved families.

Plans were made to raise the *Stanley Clipper*, tow her back to port, make the necessary repairs and return her to the fishing fleet. Salvage bags were fastened to her hull. These bags would be filled with air to raise

The Clipper being towed in the fog to the Bluff Bar, where she was lowered. — Dave Stone

her off the bottom and bring the ill-fated boat to the surface. They would then pump the water out of the hull and refloat the *Stanley Clipper*. Divers had examined the hull and found it in reasonably good shape.

On Sunday, May 20, 1984, the fishing tugs *Dover Rose*, *Ciscoette* and *Mitowmar Limited*, working in the fog, attempted to rise the vessel with airbags. Slowly she started to rise as the air was pumped in. It was an eerie sight to see the radar mast and some of the superstructure break the surface of the water. Then the top of the vessel came into view. This was as high as the *Clipper* could be raised. Its weight had been underestimated and the airbags' lifting power wasn't enough to raise her to the position where the hull could be pumped out.

She was lowered back down to the sandy bottom, where she would remain until the tugs could come back with a large crane. The tugs returned several days later with a cargomaster crane. This piece of equipment, plus the airbags had no problem raising her to the position where her hull could be pumped out. The *Stanley Clipper* was floating again and was soon towed back to Port Dover.

The company responsible for this successful operation was Can-Dive Ltd. of Toronto. This well-known diving firm has taken on numerous jobs such as this and, with their expertise, have been able to accomplish some things which had previously seemed impossible.

Practically the whole town was down at the pier that night waiting for the *Stanley Clipper* to return. *Clipper* was being towed in by the *Dover Rose*. As she came out of the darkness, one could hear the low murmur of the sombre crowd. She moved silently past like a ghost ship and came to rest at a berth nearby.

It wasn't until June 13, 1984, that the lake released the body of Captain James Saunders, southeast of Dunnville. Daryl Clement's body was found on June 26 near the Bluff Bar, a short distance from where the *Stanley Clipper* went down. John Mummery's body was found nine miles southwest of Port Dover in August 1984.

A lengthy inquest was held in Port Dover regarding the tragedy. A change in the fishing industry's often casual attitude toward safety was the key recommendation.

Port Dover, being a fishing community, has lost other vessels and crew members to the cruel waters of Long Point. However, the fishing folk of this unique hamlet are a hardy lot, like the crew of the *Stanley Clipper*. They accept the consequences of their chosen profession.

The *Stanley Clipper* is fishing again and carrying on the fine tradition established by those who sailed before her.

Toya, soon to become another dive site on Long Point.
— Dave Stone

Toya

On August 31, 1985, the sailboat *Toya* left her snug berth at Blue Bill Marina, Port Rowan, for an enjoyable trip on the lake. On board were the owner and a party of three. *Toya* had recently been built with loving care by her skipper.

As she cut across the very tip of Long Point, her keel became embedded in the bar that extends approximately half a mile from the tip. This bar changes constantly, controlled by currents and wave action. With the wave action working against the hull, the keel was soon buried and held fast by the clutching bar. There was no way to get her off. The passengers and the crew, after taking what gear they could carry, left her to her fate.

A salvager was contacted, but weather conditions made access to the site impossible. A week passed before an attempt could be made to salvage her. This attempt was unsuccessful. She had moved into shallower water, which made it difficult for the salvage boat to work, and now she was so firmly aground that she couldn't be moved. The sails and mast were all that the salvager got for his efforts. *Toya* was left to her destiny, with the lighthouse in the background standing like a large tombstone marking her grave.

The following December, Long Point was hit by a horrendous storm and *Toya* disappeared. She now lies beneath the surface, west of the bar, making her Long Point's most recent wreck, and becoming another dive site for adventurous divers in the Graveyard of the Great Lakes.

A typical schooner of yeasteryear that sailed in Long Point waters.

The Lost Schooners of Long Point

For those who have a love of ships, there is nothing more graceful than a schooner with her white sails spread to catch the breezes. In the days when schooners were at their peak, it was not unusual to see one or two of this winged fleet on the horizon. Before the steamers and the railroads, they were the nation-builders and did their job well. These vessels only had one enemy, weather conditions, which could swamp them or damage them so badly that they would be lost or stranded on a bar or beach and be pounded to pieces. Fire was not a major problem on the schooner. (The only fire aboard was in the galley, and this could be easily controlled.)

Long Point harvested a great number of these vessels. Even after the establishment of a lighthouse, the losses still remained high. The majority of these losses occurred in the late fall, the main reason being that there were many more ships and cargoes in Long Point waters at this time of year.

Losses of schooners remained high until the steel hull was introduced in the 1880s. By the turn of the century the wooden-hulled schooners were well on the decline. Many of the ships were converted to barges. It was not unusual to see three or four of these being towed down the lake by a vessel under steam power. A great number of these vessels were lost off the Point before their time, taking with them their crews and valuable cargoes. Some were vessels that had been on the lakes just a short time, while others were well past their prime. The older ones were much more prone to destruction by the ravages of the turbulent waters.

The losses of some of the schooners have been reported in previous chapters, but there were many more.

What impact did the dreaded Long Point have on the shipping industry during schooner days? Here is a brief look at some of the other schooner disasters. For a more complete picture of the vessels that were lost, consult "The Ghost Fleet of Long Point" shipwreck chart in the front of the book.

In 1827 the three-masted schooner *Ann* was caught off the tip of Long Point in a raging storm and foundered. There was only one survivor of the 23 on board.

The bottom of the lake near Gravelly Bay was covered with chestnuts when the *Oddfellow* lost her cargo after foundering in a squall. When she was lost in 1838, she was valued at $800.

Lost in the same vicinity, in 1844, was the schooner *Walsh*. She went to the bottom with all hands. Only bits and pieces of wreckage were found.

Four years later the *Uncle Tom*, one of the smaller vessels, 80 feet in length, broke up as a result of a gale. The crew made it safely to shore. The schooner had been travelling light, so there was no loss of cargo.

In 1851 the Old Cut claimed the *Billow*, a 60-foot two-master with a cargo of lumber, and the *Prince Albert*, with 35 passengers on board, all of whom made it safely to shore in the yawl boats. Both these schooners were totally destroyed.

On November 15, 1852, the schooners *Rip Van Winkle*, with a cargo of salt, and *New Haven*, carrying railroad iron, both foundered near the Old Cut. Out towards the tip, the *Sarah Eason*, carrying cheese, succumbed to the same storm.

The year 1855 spelled doom for the *Wild Rover*, a 111-foot vessel carrying a cargo of stone bound for Toronto. She was driven ashore on Long Point in a gale. Her cargo was salvaged, but in less than a week she went to pieces. Her value at the time of her loss was $10,000.

Waterlogged and loaded with a cargo of planking, the *Briget* wallowed herself to shore in 1862. She had picked up her cargo in St. Catharines and was on her way to Oswego, New York, when she ran into difficulty off Long Point. Her hull was so badly damaged that the schooner was abandoned. The crew were rescued by a passing steamer.

Floating upside down, her crew dead, the *Kate Norton* was discovered by the schooner *Dan Marble* off Long Point in 1863. The ill-fated vessel was less than a year old. She had left Toledo with 10,000 bushels of wheat in her hold. She also had a deckload of black walnut gunstocks. Overloading may have been the reason she capsized.

The *Return* ended her career that same year, when the two-masted schooner went ashore three miles west of the lighthouse. The crew were saved, but the *Return* was a complete loss.

In 1866 the 85-foot *Junius* left Toledo with a cargo of black walnut, her destination Oswego, New York. She encountered a northwest gale and started to leak. Her pumps couldn't keep ahead of the waters pouring in and she sank off the Point. Fortunately a schooner nearby was able to save the crew. The *Junius* was 15 years old when she sank.

Death struck off Long Point in the spring of 1867 when the *Merimac #2* foundered and five out of a crew of six drowned. This 115-foot three-masted schooner went to the bottom with a cargo valued at $6,000.

The *William G. Keith*, a 123-foot schooner was built and lost in 1869. Caught in a late-fall storm, she was driven near the shore. To save themselves from drowning, the crew lashed themselves in the rigging. A vessel passing nearby was unable to offer them assistance, as weather conditions placed the lives of her own crew in danger, and Long Point took the lives of five more mariners.

Another ship lost in 1869 was the *Quickstep*. At the time of her loss, the schooner had served on the lakes for 14 years. During a storm off Long Point, she collided with the schooner *Anna Hanson*. Driven by gale-force winds, they were both blown ashore near the Old Cut. The *Quickstep* was badly broken up and several attempts to salvage her failed. She was lost with a hold full of coal.

The *Zephyr* was also lost in 1869. She had sailed from Buffalo with a cargo of coal to be unloaded at Detroit. She had served the coal industry for 13 years before she foundered.

The schooners *E.S.J. Bemis* and *Mary Norton* were

both total losses during 1870. The two-masted *Bemis* had sailed the lakes for 15 years and the *Norton* for 13. The *Bemis*, with a cargo of 14,000 bushels of wheat, was being badly punished by a storm, and the captain decided to seek shelter at the Old Cut. But it was not to be. She sprang a leak approximately 15 miles from her destination and sank. The crew managed to get off before she went down. The *Mary Norton's* destruction occurred when she was forced ashore on Long Point. She was carrying a cargo of 300 tons of coal. The ship ended up a total loss.

In 1871 the *Jessie Anderson* was found with her mast protruding out of the water and her crew of eight drowned. She had been carrying a cargo of wheat. The *Resolute* also went down in 1871, taking two members of her crew with her. Her cargo of stone was also lost. That same year, the 23-year-old *Saxon* went aground and broke up.

In 1874 the *St. Andrews*, a 28-year-old veteran of the lakes, was lost while looking for the shelter of the Cut. She dropped her anchors in this area to ride out the storm, became swamped, and sunk with a cargo of 15,000 bushels of wheat. Her crew were saved.

Also in 1874, the schooner *American*, with a cargo of wheat, was driven ashore and went to pieces. An unsuccessful attempt was made to salvage the vessel. She was valued at $20,000.

The *Wanderer*, an 80-foot two-masted schooner, was caught in an 1874 fall storm and foundered. She was only valued at $3,000. The *Mockingbird*, one of the large schooners on the lakes, was also a victim that year. She was carrying coal from Buffalo to Chicago when she sprang a leak while rounding the Point, filled with water and sank. The Long Point lighthouse keeper rowed out to the stricken vessel in a small boat and rescued the crew.

Only the body of the cook and some wreckage were found when the *Belle Mitchell* disappeared in a gale in 1886. She had left Toledo on October 14 carrying a cargo of wheat bound for Buffalo. Her value was listed at $12,000.

In 1884 the *Fortune*, a 110-foot schooner, sailed out of Port Stanley carrying stove bolts. *Fortune* sprang a leak off the Point and the captain tried to save her from sinking by running her aground. The ship broke up and was a total loss. She was valued at $6,000.

Lost in 1909 was the *Sir C.T. Van Straubenzie*, a 127-foot schooner that had outlasted many of the others built in 1875. This three-masted vessel was a workhorse on the Great Lakes for 34 years. The ship was built by Louis Shickluna at St. Catharines, Ontario, and had a gross tonnage of 317 tons. The end came for the Straubenzie when it collided with the steamer *City of Erie* eight miles east of Long Point on September 27, 1909. The ill-fated vessel was bound for Cleveland, sailing out of Toronto. Three of the crew members were lost, and after the investigation, the schooner's Captain Corson was found to be negligent. The charge was made because it was proven by the Inspector of Steamships that the *Sir C.T. Van Straubenzie* did not have its starboard green light illuminated. This cleared *City of Erie* pilot Edward S. Pickell of any blame.

The *Dinah*, a small vessel running from Hamilton, Ontario, to Port Stanley, Ontario, was lost in 1910. She was caught in a storm off Long Point and became a total loss. Her value was $5,000.

In 1917 the large 264-foot three-masted schooner *Magnetic* broke in two and sank with a cargo of iron ore. The crew were saved by the vessel towing her.

Many of the years not listed in this chapter also had schooner calamities with loss of life and property. They can be seen on the chart in the front of the book. In addition to the schooner losses, there were losses of brigantines, barques, sidewheelers, wooden steam screw propellors, barges and steel-hulled vessels. The tragic stories of some of these are told in the previous chapters.

Regardless of how well vessels were constructed, many were no match for the merciless waters off Long Point.

Contraband

With Long Point stretching nearly halfway across Lake Erie, it made an ideal location for smugglers and rumrunners to ply their profession. The shelter of the bay, depending on the weather conditions, made a perfect rendezvous for those who wished to engage in this illicit business. Also assisting them were the channels on the north side, where they could hide from the law and those who objected strongly to the business in which these entrepreneurs were engaged.

During the era of "The Great National Thirst," which came about in the United States by the passing of the Volstead Act, prohibiting the manufacture, importation and drinking of any kind of spirits, there was one commodity responsible for more fast boat trips across the lake than anything else on the market: good Canadian whisky.

Liquor was not to be exported from Canada to the United States, but there was one way to overcome this situation. Smuggle it. This created a new industry and gave employment to many. There was money to be made, but the business had its drawbacks: there was no job security, no hospitalization plan and no pension. Also, one couldn't expect to get a bonus for long service, as in many cases employees didn't live that long.

One plus for rumrunning was that no one had to worry about the expense of a funeral. If you were caught in the middle of the lake by the U.S. Coast Guard and you didn't stop when they shot across your bow, they simply blew you and the boat out of the water. To protect themselves from the bullets of the Coast Guard, a number of rumrunning boats were installed with armour plating topside.

A trick of the rumrunning trade was to place the bottles in weighted jute bags. If the runners' boat was about to be apprehended by the enemy, the bags

The Grey Ghost, an armour-plated rumrunner, blown up with $12,000 worth of whisky on board.

would be thrown overboard. If this was done close to shore, they could be picked up later. But thrown out in deep water, they were a complete loss. Some of these bottles eventually made it to shore. The bag would rot and the wave action would bring some up on the beach. You can imagine the joy that would overcome a parched whisky lover when he stumbled across one of these bottles. Brand preference didn't much matter.

Shelley Cook, a lighthouse keeper who spent 31 years tending the Long Point light, told of how the rumrunners used to bother him. They would demand the use of his telephone, claiming they were fishermen having engine problems with their boat. Others claimed that they had too many fish on board and that they had to call their fishing company to send out another boat to assist in bringing in their catch. To fool the keeper they would keep their boat out of sight and approach the lighthouse on foot.

One such case occurred when a so-called fisherman said he had to call Port Dover, but the call was made to the American side. Soon after the stranger left, a craft appeared rounding the Point. Much to the surprise of Mr. Cook, it wasn't the typical type of commercial fish-

104

More than one rumrunner ended up in Davey Stone's locker.

ing boat used out of Port Dover. The boat he saw was a low sleek craft travelling at a great speed towards Erie, Pennsylvania.

Keeper Cook became wise to their ways and soon learned to assess the situation and differentiate between those in need and rumrunners.

Mrs. Lorne Brown, whose husband replaced Shelley Cook as lighthouse keeper in the summer of 1928, related the following story to me years ago. One evening she and her husband went for a walk down south beach. Mr. Brown loved nature and when off duty he would explore this wilderness. After they had walked some distance, with the sun setting, they decided it was time to head back to the lighthouse. As they turned around and started back, Mr. Brown spotted what he thought was a log about a hundred yards offshore, appearing then disappearing in a slight swell. They continued their walk, but had only gone a short distance when curiosity overcame the lighthouse keeper. Being an excellent swimmer — he had been a member

of the crew of the lifesaving station before joining the army — he shed some clothes and swam out to the log.

But it wasn't a log. It was the body of a fully clothed man who hadn't been in the water long. This time, however, the waters of Long Point couldn't be blamed for the death. Bullet holes are not one of the symptoms of death by drowning. It is presumed that this person was disposed of by a rival rumrunner.

It was during this period of prohibition that the crew of the rumrunner *Anna* nearly met their end. While running their cargo across the lake their boat developed engine trouble. Unable to get it started, the crew spent two weeks adrift. Eventually their boat drifted to shore near the end of Long Point.

Another story relating to the transporting of contraband goes like this. The fishing tug *Dover Rose* was trawling for smelt east of Long Point. In charge of the commercial fishing vessel was Captain Lloyd Kenline. The long trawl net became caught on an obstruction on the bottom of the lake. The net was brought to the surface, and in the net was discovered a large section of a hull from a wooden boat. In the hull section was a 24-horsepower gasoline "Buffalo" engine, a drive shaft and a bronze propeller. The tugs *Stuart B.* and *Ciscoe* were signalled by Captain Kenline to assist him in bringing this 30-foot hull to Port Dover.

After the hull was returned to port and examined, some speculated that it was the remains of a rumrunner from prohibition days, as it was one of the type of boats that were very popular on Lake Erie during that era.

Whether this particular boat was lost by actions of the Coast Guard, a rival, fire or weather is not known. On more than one occasion these carriers of "instant joy" mysteriously disappeared. But happily for our neighbours to the south, many of them also made it.

Waterford District High School students and staff trying to raise the marker in 1985.

Destination Long Point — Not by Ship But by Boat

Four individuals have successfully walked across the frozen lake from the United States to Long Point, Ontario.

Others have tried it. Some started out but turned back after several hours walking. Some who attempted were reported missing. At a great expense to United States and Canadian taxpayers, search parties and aircraft were called out, and these missing adventurers were located and returned to the point of embarkation.

Two men who received a great deal of publicity for walking from the American shores to the Long Point lighthouse were Walter Lick, 1912, and Gene Hauser, 1963.

Lick left a village in northern Pennsylvania on February 13, 1912. Nineteen-year-old Lick covered a distance of 25 miles to reach the lighthouse at the end of Long Point.

One can imagine the shock lighthouse keeper William Porritt had when he answered a knock on his door and there stood Lick, whose first words were "How far is Port Rowan?" He spent the night at the keeper's house. The next morning, refreshed, he went on his way.

He travelled safely across the bay. With his destination close at hand, disaster struck and nearly ended it all. Close to the harbour of Port Rowan were areas where the ice had been recently harvested. The skim ice broke through and in he went. Fortunately there were people nearby to haul him out.

Lick has become one of Long Point's legends. To commemorate his feat, a cement marker was placed immediately east of the base of the lighthouse. There it remained until high water toppled it over into the pond. It was buried forever when the base of the lighthouse was filled in during the reinforcement and res-

The marker commemorating Walter Lick's feat put there by the lighthouse keeper shortly after Lick's long walk.

toration program by the federal government in 1987.

Fifty-one years after Walter Lick's adventure, Gene Heuser, 32, of Harbour Creek, Pennsylvania, stepped on the ice at Shades Harbour, Pennsylvania, Pennsylvania, at 8 a.m., Saturday, March 2, 1963. He carried a flashlight, compass, and a large willow staff, which he used to assist him during the rough walk and to test the ice ahead. He encountered snowdrifts 15 feet high and slabs of ice five feet high. He walked 20 miles out of his way to avoid several stretches of open water, piles of snow and large ice mounds.

He finally reached Long Point lighthouse at 8 a.m., Sunday. He had been on the treacherous journey for 24 hours. It had taken 12 hours longer than Walter Lick's trip. When he arrived at the Point, he encountered some Canadian scientists who at first just couldn't believe his story.

Clayton Scofield, the lighthouse keeper, took him in and looked after his needs. The next day he was driven down to Port Rowan, by way of the beach, to the highway.

Clayton Scofield, retired lighthouse keeper, with the willow staff Heuser used to assist himself during his walk across the lake.

This chapter would not be complete without mentioning that during 1977 two men from Erie, Pennsylvania, walked across the lake to the Canadian shores. There is some local folklore concerning the event. The story goes that these men had been reported missing. Search parties were sent out, but were unsuccessful in locating them. The two fearless adventurers were finally discovered in one of the local beverage rooms on the Canadian side.

The First Lighthouse on Long Point

The greatest fear of the early mariners sailing in Lake Erie was Long Point. Sailing in these waters by day in a storm was bad enough, but at night, with no light to guide them, it was a terror.

As the list of disasters grew, people on both sides of the lake applied pressure to the authorities to get something done. The first steps were taken in 1803 by the Legislature of Upper Canada. To raise revenue for lighthouses, a three-pence-per-ton duty was levied on all vessels entering an Upper Canada port. The monies collected were to be used for the construction and maintenance of lighthouses. Only two lighthouses, one at York, the other at Niagara, were built before 1812.

In 1817 the need for a lighthouse at Long Point was brought before the Legislature. The representative for Norfolk County, Colonel Robert Nichol, looked into this matter immediately. The Legislature approved of his ideas, but the sitting of the sessions was closing, so no further development occurred at that time.

As the year went by, the Americans lost more and more vessels. They wanted some action taken immediately to prevent this increasing loss of life and property. In 1828 they pressed the British government to build a lighthouse. If the British wouldn't, they wanted permission to build one themselves. They were desperate.

This message was sent to England and eventually came back to the Lieutenant-Governor of Upper Canada. Action was taken in 1829 and £1,000 were appropriated by the Legislature to construct a lighthouse at the end of Long Point.

The site of the first lighthouse built on Long Point, 1830, showing the remains of the foundation. — Dave Stone

Three commissioners were appointed: Duncan McCall, Francis Walsh and Thomas Cross. Plans were made immediately to get construction under way. Specifications for the project were completed and tenders were let.

The tender of Joseph Van Norman and Brothers, Normandale, was accepted, at £925, to construct the building and install the light.

The Van Normans constructed a round stone tower, 50 feet from the base to the platform below the light. The foundation was 30 feet square. They installed five windows of two lights each. The tower also had a winding stair with two platforms. The lantern above the platform was 8½ feet in diameter. The 12 lamps had glass tubes and 16-inch reflectors. To hold these lamps, a chandelier was put in place.

From November 3, 1830, on, the mariners sailing in Long Point waters had a light to guide them away from this threatening shoal.

Another £100 was obtained from the authorities to erect a house for the light-keeper, pay his salary, and supply wicks and oil for the lamp. The first keeper was

Thomas Price, who was paid the sum of one dollar a day for his services.

During 1832 the north shore of the Point eroded badly. The next year the base was reinforced, but this did not stop the pounding waves from damaging the structure. Construction was begun on a different site, and in 1843 the second lighthouse was built.

One would have great difficulty finding the remains of this first lighthouse. This site today is approximately one mile from the tip of the Point, at the edge of the evergreens, some distance from the north shore. Finding the site, now behind rolling dunes, it is hard to imagine that it was destroyed by water action.

The second lighthouse, built on Long Point in 1843. — Mrs. Lorne Brown

The Second Lighthouse

The second lighthouse was built in 1843 and was an entirely different structure than the first one. It was 70 feet in in height, including the lantern house. The light was comprised of 16 burners and wicks and originally burned whale oil. Then, for economy, it was transferred over to coal oil in 1864. This light could be seen for 13 miles. Later on, precision ground lenses were installed so that much more available light could be seen offshore by the passing ships.

This lighthouse operated for 73 years, and then it too fell victim to the ravages of the lake. It was replaced by the present lighthouse, which started operating in May 1916.

The second lighthouse stood for many years afterwards on the edge of the shoreline. For some time it was used as a lookout or observation post by the crew members of the Long Point lifesaving station. During or after a storm they would look out from this high

Part of the foundation and rods of the second lighthouse back in the late 1960s. — Dave Stone

perch to see if any ships were in trouble. Often times, when a crew member ascended, the old building would creak and shake. Finally an order was given in 1929 to burn it down, so lighthouse keeper did so.

Fears that it might become a hazard to navigation have been confirmed today. Since the erosion of the north shore, the reinforcing rods which were once on the beach are now well offshore. The rods are just below the surface of the water, and the lighthouse keepers have marked these with a buoy. I too have put them on when no markers were showing. If these rods were hit by an unsuspecting boater, they would tear the bottom of the craft wide open.

The Third Lighthouse

The third lighthouse was started in 1915 and completed in 1916. It is a reinforced concrete, tapered octagonal tower rising to 102 feet, including tower and housing for the light. Around the foundation they constructed a 36-foot side cobble apron, later replaced by a concrete clab.

An accurate description of the building of this structure can only be assumed. The original drawings of the lighthouse are available, but those showing the actual construction were lost.

At the top of the lighthouse is a 400-watt mercury vapour light encased by prisms. It is visible from Erie, Pennsylvania. This is much more effective than the original light installed when the lighthouse was first built. Covering only a distance of 14 miles, this original light was 100,000 candle power. Fuel for the light was vapourized petroleum. This light had to be watched closely by the light-keepers to ensure that it would not fail.

To make the light rotate, a clockwork mechanism was used. It was run by two large weights and wound up to the top every 8 hours. It was like a giant timepiece.

An amusing story from Bill Ansley, former head lighthouse keeper, relates how he and his assistant would keep in shape.

When he first went on the station, the weights still had to be wound. To see which keeper could wind the weights faster, a contest was developed. Nearing the end of an eight-hour period, both keepers would step outside, one with a stopwatch, the other preparing himself for a record-breaking sprint. Go! The challenger would run as fast as he could across the lengthy catwalk, into the lighthouse, up the steep steps two at a time to the top, there to wind the weights as fast as possible, then grab the handrails and slide down the flight of steps without touching them. Once to the bottom, he would make a mad dash over the catwalk to the timekeeper holding the stopwatch.

At the lighthouse in the late 1970s. The keeper's house still has some beach in front of it. — Dave Stone

The winners varied from season to season, but Bill must have been the winner on many occasions, since he outlasted all the light-keepers that started with him throughout the years, beginning in 1955. In 1984 Bill Ansley retired as a light-keeper after spending 29 years at Long Point and six at Niagara-on-the-Lake. His father also had been a lighthouse keeper.

Over the years there have been major changes. In the early forties there was the conversion from steam to oil. During the late 1950s new diesel engines and generators were installed. The vapour light was changed to a 1,500-watt incandescent lamp. The weights no longer had to be wound, as the lenses were now turned by an electric motor.

In 1963 the light was changed once more, to a 400-watt mercury light.

Bill Ansley, lighthouse keeper for 29 years at Long Point, beside the prism lens. — Dave Stone

The lighthouse at night. — Dave Stone

When this building was torn down, I volunteered to bring a load of the old bricks from the end of the Point to the mainland by boat. Bill Ansley, the light-keeper, was going to use them for a fireplace he planned to build. Water conditions were ideal, so we loaded my boat up, having no concern about a rough passage.

The house finally succumbed to the ravages of high water in 1983. This building was sold and removed from the Point by barge. — Dave Stone

I left the tip around 4 p.m., running at low speed. By the time I reached the outer buoy, water conditions had started to change and the wind had picked up. There was no way I could go on the inside of the bar with such a heavy load.

The weather worsened. With waves breaking over the bow, I was taking on some water. I could see my boat filling up and literally sinking like a ton of bricks. My thoughts immediately were to throw the bricks overboard, but there were so many of them. I started the bilge pump and headed into the waves. The boat responded as if it had a displacement hull instead of a planing one. I could see that as long as the wave action didn't worsen, I would make it.

Several hours later, soaked and cold, I made it to my boathouse. I kept a couple of bricks from the cargo to remind me that bricks and stones don't float.

The old fog station, built in 1900. When these powerful horns sounded, the surrounding grass would flatten out. — Harry B. Barrett

The same building surrounded by water and in disrepair. Since this picture was taken, the old fog station has completely fallen in. — Dave Stone

The engine room and fog station in use today. In 1987 the building in the foreground was removed from the Point. — Dave Stone

The Old Cut lighthouse in the days when it was still in operation. — George Perry

The Old Cut Lighthouse

This lighthouse was built in 1879 to replace the lightship that marked the Cut. This structure was considerably different than those built on the end of the Point. The living accommodations for the keepers were incorporated right in the lighthouse. Built on a stone foundation, the walls and upper structure were

How the Old Cut lighthouse looks today under private ownership. — Dave Stone

made of wood. It was located on the east side of the Cut. The total height of the tapered tower and the lantern house was 60 to 65 feet. The white light would tell sailors 12 miles away about the entrance to the Cut.

In 1906 Long Point was battered by a severe storm, the Cut was filled in and ceased to exist. The lighthouse continued to operate, marking part of this shoal of Long Point until it closed down in 1916.

This lighthouse and surrounding land was sold by the government to a private owner. One of the previous owners was T.H. Hancock of Toronto. The present owner of this historical lighthouse is Mr. Ewart Ostrander, a well-known resident of Tillsonburg and Long Point.

What is the future of this 108-year-old navigational landmark? It is one of the few lighthouses in Canada receiving an abundance of traffic right by its front door. Its location is on the highway immediately west of the Long Point Provincial Park. I believe this building would make an excellent interpretive centre and museum in conjunction with the provincial park.

Let's hope that in the years ahead "the lighthouse the lake forgot" doesn't go the way of a number of other Canadian historical structures.

How the lighthouse will look in the future, after the painting scaffolds are gone. — Dave Stone

Attempts Made to Keep the Lighthouse Shining

Lighthouses across the continent have been destroyed by hurricanes, violent storms, fires, explosions, high waters and erosion. To save the present Long Point lighthouse from the fate of its two predecessors — lost by high water and erosion — the federal government implemented plans to save it from the encroaching waters. With the rapid recession on the north shore, especially in the immediate vicinity of the lighthouse, something had to be done.

In 1978, after a study of erosion conditions along the north shore, a project was developed to assist in protecting and building up this shoreline. A construction crew arrived at the lighthouse that year, complete with front-end loader, cement mixer, tons of bagged cement, and other equipment and supplies necessary to complete this project.

The project entailed the construction and placement of a series of groins running at right angles to the north beach and out into the lake a short distance. It was hoped that these groins would stop the recession of the north shore. Snow fences were also positioned on the beach to help stabilize and hold the sand. Large sausage-like nylon bags were put into position and filled with cement by the construction crew. They ran from the edge of the beach out into the water. At the time of construction these tubes were partly above the surface.

This attempt was unsuccessful and water levels continued to rise, resulting in the washout of sand where it joined the beach. In a few years they were all covered with water and now have disappeared from view.

Boaters should exercise extreme caution when

*Aerial view showing them
all in position in the
lighthouse vicinity.*
— *Dave Stone*

approaching the north beach in the vicinity of the lighthouse because of these submerged objects.

After the devastating storm of December 2, 1985, and because of continuing high water levels, there was concern for the operation and safety of the lighthouse. In 1986 an engineering study was made of the lighthouse. Local rumours circulated that the lighthouse was on tilt! This was not so. It was found plumb and showed no signs of distress. Then a more detailed structural inspection was undertaken to check the soundness of the concrete in the structure and its base. Proposals resulted from the engineering studies and an action plan was implemented to save the lighthouse from being destroyed by the storms and high water levels. The plan included restoring it to its original look with the exception of some modifications that had to be made to repair it and prepare it for automation.

In May 1987 Canadian Dredge and Dock Company of Toronto arrived at the lighthouse with construction workers, a bulldozer, several cranes, front-end loader, a barge and a tug. Around the base of the lighthouse they drove 32-foot steel piling to a depth of 27 feet. Sand was transported from the very tip of the Point, the only place it could be taken from since the dunes and other areas could not be disturbed. Using this sand, the base was filled in to a foot below the top of the exposed pilings, then wetted and packed down.

Nu Carl, another construction company and subcontractor, put a foot of concrete on top of the two cells, or circles, which were now around the base and filled with sand. Each of these two circles are 75 feet in diameter. One of these circles is a helicopter pad.

The same contractor demolished the entrance to the lighthouse, and filled the first floor was five feet of sand and one of concrete. A new entrance was cut

The new doorway being replaced to match the original one, vintage 1916. — Dave Stone

The new helicopter pad. — Dave Stone

through, resembling exactly the old entrance. All the bad spots and cold joints were chipped on the structure and filled with a special adhesive. Sandblasting and painting followed.

From information received on the site in the fall of 1987, I understand that plans are in place to automate this lighthouse by 1990. Solar panels will be used and a cold-start generator will be installed to take over when there is no sun. Three hundred and fifty-six 6- and 12-volt storage batteries are required for the solar system. All of this equipment will be on the new first floor. The second and third levels will be used as accommodation for technicians if necessary when checking or repairing equipment. The radio beam, which now operates in a sequence, will become a continuous beam.

Since 1916 this lighthouse has been sending out four beams of light across the lake. It casts a beam of light every eight seconds. It has been doing this for 71 years. But no more. With the amount of vibration that occurred to the lighthouse during the reconstruction program, one of the large prisms came loose from its support, fell out, and was smashed to pieces. I understand that these prisms were made in France during the period when the lighthouse was built. Replacement today could be rather difficult, so this blank spot is now covered with a piece of sheet metal. With solar lighting to be installed in the near future, this type of lens will no longer be required.

So now the old Long Point light is sending out three beams of light instead of four to those who travel in these waters. What would some of the old schooner captains think?

The lifesaving station and crew members with the self-bailing, self-righting lifeboat.
— *Mrs. Lorne Brown*

The Long Point Lifesaving Station

Even with one lighthouse at the end of the Point and the other marking the Old Cut, it was deemed necessary by the Ministry of Marine and Fisheries to install a lifesaving station on Long Point. During 1883 a station was built on the south shore, just west of the Old Cut lighthouse.

Prior to the erection of this station, the hope of being rescued from shore was just that, a hope. Ships in distress and endangered mariners were rescued only by chance. With no patrol on the beach, no permanent crew to render assistance, and no lifeboat, the victims were at the mercy of the lake, usually resulting in the loss of life and property.

This station, the fifth to be built on the Great Lakes, was not what could be called a refuge station. These stations were simply well provisioned, under the charge of one keeper only, and the type that could be used where the nature of the coast makes escape from stranded vessels comparatively easy — the main dangers to seafarers here being less the chance of drowning than the likelihood of perishing due to exposure and hunger after reaching shore.

Because of the violent nature of Long Point, with such a record of death and destruction, a fully manned station with a lifeboat and other lifesaving devices was required.

The 25-foot lifeboat used to rescue those in peril was self-bailing and self-righting. A crew of seven oarsmen and a coxswain were required to man it efficiently.

Not only was the crew required to maintain the station and boat, and to spend time in the observation posts, but they also had to patrol the beach.

The station crew would patrol the beach some distance each side of the station at regular intervals between sunset and sunrise. If the weather was foggy, the patrol would be continued throughout the day. A patrolman discovering a vessel standing in danger would signal the ship to warn it off or, should the vessel be aground, let her crew know that they were dis-

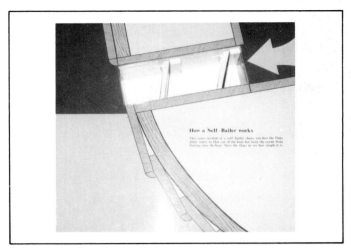

How a self-bailer works. The flaps allow the water to flow out but keep water from flowing in. — Dave Stone

Lady guests visiting the crew members of the lifesaving station near the Cut. — Mrs. Lorne Brown

Boathouse and crew's quarters, observation tower and captain's residence at the end of the Point, north shore. — Mrs. Lorne Brown

covered and assistance was at hand.

The station served its purpose well, rescuing ship-wrecked sailors, stranded vessels and cargoes at the Old Cut.

When the channel filled in and was no longer of use, the station was moved to the south shore at the end of Long Point. For several years it operated at this new location, but because of its exposed location on this beach, subject to the prevailing winds from the south-west, launching of the lifeboat was difficult. (Ironically the hull of an old wrecked steamer was used to hold the beach in front of the station. But the hull ran parallel with the shore instead of at right angles to it, and the water washed between them, so the station had to be moved to the north shore.)

The station at the end of the Point had a building to house the boat and the oarsmen. The captain had his own residence for himself and his family. To launch the boat, a track ran from the boathouse to the water's edge with a flatbed car carrying the boat.

The following is a typical example of how the crew responded during a marine crisis off the Point:

A member of the crew, upon discovering a ship in distress while on patrol or atop the observation tower, hastened to the station for assistance. If the use of the boat was practical, it was launched from its carriage.

The difficulties of rescue by operations from shore were greatly increased when the anchors of the stricken vessels had been let go after entering the breakers — as was frequently done — and the chances of saving lives were correspondingly lessened.

All that is left of the Long Point lifesaving station. — Dave Stone

When the boat reached the vessel, the captain of the lifesaving station directed the crew. Women, children and helpless persons were taken on board the lifeboat first. No goods or baggage were taken off until all were safely ashore. Any goods placed in the lifeboat without the captain's authority were thrown overboard. Once the survivors were all on the beach, the lifeboat returned to the vessel to try to save property or cargo. This was only done when there was no threat of loss of life while making the return trip.

There were also occasions when weather conditions were so bad that the lifeboat could not safely reach a grounded ship. In this case a breeches buoy had to be employed. A shot with a small line attached was fired over the ship. Then, with a heavier line and a block attached, the breeches buoy was fastened and the victims brought ashore in this apparatus.

The men of the Long Point lifesaving station were separated from their loved ones for months on end, suffering many hardships in the line of duty. On numerous occasions they risked their lives to save another's. Their feats of bravery and courage will always be remembered.

With the days of sail fading away and with much larger ships on the lakes, the value of the lifesaving station diminished. In 1926 the crew were dispersed and the station shut down. Gone now are the frame buildings that housed the lifeboat and crew, only several cement abutments remain, monuments to a humanitarian service that lasted 43 years.

THE LIFEBOAT

"Man the lifeboat!" loudly they cry,
   I know that call right well,
Thou ark of mercy, how shall I
   Thy deeds of Glory tell?

When, with my comrades brave and true,
   We launch upon the wave,
To rescue some shipwrecked crew,
   Whose lives we seek to save.

What though tempestuous winds may roar,
   And angry waves assail,
We pull still stronger with the oar,
   Regardless of the gale.

And though the storm King's forces do
   Their utmost to defeat,
We'll reach the wreck, take off the crew,
   And make our work complete.

God bless the lifeboat and her crew,
   And may they ever be
Faithful and true, their work to do
   Like heroes of the sea.

Captain W. D. Andrews, 1890

The cross on the very tip of Long Point, 1965.

The Cross at the End of Long Point

In 1965 a large cross, made out of an 18-foot cedar four by four and fastened together with a large brass bolt from the keel of a wrecked boat, was erected at the end of Long Point.

Reverend Herring of Port Rowan and his driver, Ed Garvey, tied the cross and the two pedestals to a jeep and took the long adventurous journey along the lakeshore, sometimes half in and half out of the water, sometimes labouring in soft sand. They found the loneliness and the grandeur of the scenery fascinating, the beach strewn with flotsam and jetsam. The driver was alert at all times for obstacles on the beach. An accident or breakdown out here could be life-threatening.

The lighthouse eventually came into view. They passed it and came upon a spit of sand "where the two seas meet." The cross was placed overlooking the lake and the bay, and facing a natural hollow in the grassy dunes. The following Sunday a service was held. Approximately 30 people were in attendance. They came by boat and jeep. Those on duty at the lighthouse were also in attendance with their families.

What a fitting place to have this wilderness chapel. The screaming gulls, the wild solitude of the windswept sand dunes, the whitecaps in the bay, the cross so lonely and primitive. One could stand there and pause to reflect on those unfortunate souls who came to their end off Long Point.

A few years later, high water threatened this site, and Bill Ansley, the lighthouse keeper, moved it to higher ground. However, during the high water of 1982 this second site was washed out and the cross no longer stands.

121

Remains of a once proud vessel that reached its "Last Port of Call."

This hull came ashore near the breakwater after a violent storm in 1981. — Dave Stone

Shipwrecks and Artifacts Ashore

Most of the shipwrecks are located in the deeper waters surrounding this sandspit of Long Point. However, there are also some that have come up on the beach. They were transported there by severe fall or spring storms, probably buried in a sandbar not too far from shore and washed out by the wave action.

During the summer of 1969 I discovered a wreck in a most unusual place. On the south beach, behind a large sand dune, I found approximately 82 feet of ship wreckage. There was a complete outline of the remaining hull. Rusted metal fittings, drifts and spikes were still there, where they had been fastened to the vessel.

Julia Stone, the author's daughter, with a block and small deadeye. Both these articles were located between the beach and sandbar off south shore. — Dave Stone

This one had come to rest approximately six miles west of the lighthouse, south beach. — Dave Stone

The boneyard at Port Dover. Parts of lost ships' hulls which have been caught in the commercial fishermen's nets off Long Point. — Dave Stone

More wreckage on the beach at Long Point, 1975. — Dave Stone

Ninety-six feet of hull that was completely buried in the sand near the Big Blow Out. — Dave Stone

Ships are not the only vessels caught in the raging fury of Long Point waters. Above is a stranded three-holer outhouse with one survivor. Tim Knight on board. — Dave Stone

What was this ship doing behind a dune and a considerable distance from the lake?

Probably about 130 years ago the vessel laid near the water's edge. Eventually, as water levels dropped, a dune was formed between the wreck and the water's edge. As the dune built, the wreck became hidden from view. I have been back to this location a number of times but have not been able to see the remains, since the dune has completely covered the wreck with sand.

When part of the timbers of the hull are carried to the edge of the beach, a sandbar starts to build. Going back to the same area a month or so later, one would likely find the wreck completely buried. It would stay this way until a severe storm's wave action washed the sand away, once again exposing it to view.

With the vast amount of shipwreck remains I have seen here over the past 35 years, it is quite clear how Long Point got its title as "Graveyard of the Great Lakes."

Canadian Wildlife Service

Long Point Company

Treasure-Seeking Today, on and off Long Point

Looking for treasure on Long Point is impossible today, as there is no way one can get permission for this type of venture.

A very large tract of Long Point land and marsh is owned by the Government of Canada and is under the capable management of the Canadian Wildlife Service. This 3,200-hectare tract is classified as a National Wildlife Area and is well posted and patrolled. Trespassers have been prosecuted. Also, under the National Wildlife Area regulations, "removing, damaging or defacing an artifact is prohibited."

Another portion of Long Point, 3,000 hectares and Ryerson Island, is in private ownership, belonging to the Long Point Company. This area is also well patrolled and posted, with no trespassing allowed. This applies not only to the interior, but also the beaches. One exception to this is that public swimming has been premitted on the east side of Ryerson Island.

Nature, too, has eliminated the possibility of finding anything placed or washed up on the beaches. High water levels over the years have washed out thousands of hectares of shoreline, removing sand dunes, trees and any type of artifact that might have been buried there. This point was well made in 1984, during a survey by William A. Fox of Indian archaeological sites. Fox believed that a considerable number of these sites had been washed out, and those that might still be left were in danger of being lost forever. Since that time water levels have reached an all-time high and these sites have indeed disappeared.

If you are seriously inclined to search for offshore treasure, be it of monetary value or perhaps just an old shipwreck with its cargo still on board, the following simple steps must be taken.

Spend the next ten years doing research about the shipwrecks around Long Point. This way you will have an idea where to search. It's a big lake, and if you miss what you're looking for by a metre, you might as well have missed it by ten kilometres.

Take a diving course and be prepared to pay at least $3,000 for the latest diving equipment. Second-hand gear can be bought for less, but be sure you know what you are buying. A good diving work boat can be purchased for $200,000. Side scan sonar is a necessity, along with loran and other navigational equipment. To keep those dive tanks filled, an air compressor will be required.

To document your find, a good underwater camera plus lighting equipment will be necessary. For $3,000 one can take some excellent pictures.

If married, one must have an understanding wife or husband, particularly if she or he is a non-diver. You will need to justify all the time spent away from home and to somehow sell your spouse on the idea that all the money being spent looking for the wreck is for her or his benefit. It is also very important that you have a job that will support both your family and your addiction for shipwrecks.

Be prepared to spend weekends, holidays and even take time off from work for the endless search. And many, many days you'll get no rewards for your efforts.

But there are rewards. An old schooner or steamer may be found — but one must remember these were not carrying pirates' gold or other plunder, but only the staple commodities used by the early settlers in the area, products such as wool, hides, salt, rock, grain, lumber, coal or other goods that were required for day-to-day living.

Let's say plenty of research, documentation and endless searching have given you your prize. The wreck has been located, loaded with artifacts and some cargo. Just because you have found the wreck doesn't mean that it's yours. If you start salvaging or removing artifacts, there is a chance of being fined up to $10,000.

Under the federal laws protecting shipwrecks exists a Part 10 of the Canada Shipping Act that gives the Canadian Coast Guard's Receiver of Wrecks the authority to act as a custodian of a shipwreck. The Receiver's role is to protect the rightful owner — which could be a shipping company, an individual owner or an insurance company — against any unauthorized salvaging for up to one year. He then returns it to the rightful owners. However, if no owner can be located in a year's time, the Receiver can reimburse the salvor and dispose of the wreck through a sale directed by the Minister of Transport. If an owner is located, he must pay all administrative fees for the Coast Guard and expenses for the salvor's effort and risk. For payment of cases involving small vessels and nominal expenses, the Receiver determines the amount. For larger vessels these cases must be settled by the Federal Court of Canada, which acts as Admiralty Court in this country.

The provincial laws are different. They state that everything on the bottom belongs to the province. Some provinces, to protect wreck sites, have designated these as heritage sites, making it illegal to remove anything from such vessels.

To do any archaeological field work on a wreck, a licence must be issued by the Ministry of Culture and Communications. This comes under section 48 of the Heritage Act. A proper reporting procedure to the Ministry is also part of the conditions of the licence.

To considerably cut your costs on sophisticated underwater searching equipment, use a wreck-sniffing dog named "Sea-weed"! — Dave Stone

Retrieval of artifacts from the wreck can only be carried out with the provision of adequate conservation measures and in consultation with the Minister of Culture and Communications' regional archaeologist. There are those who ignore these regulations, but they run the risk of paying a large fine.

A number of provinces are now putting pressure on both federal and provincial governments for tougher legislation to protect the wrecks.

All the research, searching and legal entanglement is enough to turn some hopefuls off. To others it is a challenging experience, and there are rewards.

In my opinion, the greatest reward in finding a ship-wreck is not its monetary value but its historical significance. When I look at a wreck I don't see a large pile of twisted planking, machinery scattered in the bowels of the vessel, or a broken spar lying nearby. What I see is a time capsule from an era long ago.

Many people think that when a diver locates a wreck, there it sits, completely intact, upright and looking as good as it did the day it sank. This is not so in most cases. Unless one knows something about ship construction, the wreck may look like a cluttered building site, with bits and pieces everywhere. But in a wreck are the artifacts that our forefathers used in traversing the lakes.

When observing a wreck, one might be looking at a graveyard, the last resting place of those who lost their lives when the ill-fated vessel went down. Lying nearby in the wreckage might be the remains of some unfortunate victim. Therefore, this wreck should be treated with the same respect as a cemetery.

As to the vessel, conservation is the aim of most divers and archaeologists today. Wreck stripping, removing artifacts, whether a cup or a large anchor, is considered totally unacceptable by the diving community.

A great number of wrecks in the whole Great Lakes system have been completely stripped. The only things left are what couldn't be removed and brought to the surface. These historical treasures are lost forever.

I feel that if a wreck has an artifact on it of historical significance, and there is a danger that it could be lost or damaged, it should be brought up, preserved and placed in a museum. But before it is removed, it should be drawn and photographed to document where it was located on the vessel and its function.

The real rewards or treasures are the photographs taken of the wreck and the artifacts on board. This way our heritage is captured for posterity. Not only can these photographs be used for research purposes, but they can be put on view for all to see. This method of treasure-hunting is much more meaningful than pulling a wreck apart at random for some goody.

The real treasure waiting for you off Long Point is our marine heritage.

There have been countless number of shipwrecks throughout man's history. These tragedies occur when a ship becomes involved in a sinking, foundering, fire, stranding, explosion or collision.

According to research that I've done, with the material that was available, 626 lives were lost through marine disasters off Long Point between 1814 and 1984. I'm sure that there were some vessels lost that went unrecorded. These unknown numbers would make this awesome list even greater.

Even with the construction of lighthouses and the operation of a lifesaving station during that time period, the Point still created havoc for the mariner, mainly due to weather conditions.

It can be appreciated, when looking at these numbers, why the name Long Point struck terror in the hearts of men. In so many cases the loss of a vessel included the loss of the whole crew. In many cases these men were all from the same town or village. Whole communities mourned.

Even though there are no longer wooden sail and steam vessels plying the waters off Long Point, disasters still occur, involving people in pleasure boats, sports fishermen and duck hunters. Most of these losses happen in the inner or outer bay of Long Point.

Over the years I have been involved in several needle-in-the-haystack searches for missing persons. In one case, in October 1963, a fishing party of four in a small boat disappeared. Articles belonging to the missing four were found on the Point and the overturned boat was located by the Ontario Provincial Police, who spotted it from an aircraft. The boat was 11 miles from where it had been launched at the Old Cut.

This was one of the most intensive searches made on and off Long Point. The search party was made up of Provincial Police, Ministry of Natural Resources personnel, R.C.M.P., volunteer firemen, other volunteers, and 45 officers and men of the Royal Canadian Regiment.

One of the missing men was a member of the regiment from London, Ontario. The R.C.R. set up headquarters on Courtright Ridge, then searched the entire peninsula on foot, looking for their missing comrade and his companions.

Offshore 20 boats worked back and forth in the area where the four were supposedly lost. Overhead search planes kept checking the shoreline of the Point for clues.

The search was at times hindered by rough waters and bad weather, but as soon as things settled down, out we went again.

After 11 days of searching, three of the missing victims' bodies were found. The next day the fourth was located.

This long search was headed by Harvey Ferris of Long Point.

On another occasion, during the evening of August 18, 1970, I was returning to Long Point from Turkey Point when I spotted another boat speeding towards me. It was Ted Whitworth, who ran a marina at Long Point. He said he had come across a 28-foot cruiser drifting aimlessly in the bay. He had boarded the cruiser and found a man in shock. Ted finally got a story out of him on what was going on. He had gone for a cruise in the bay with the owner of the boat. The owner had gone out on the bow to adjust a windshield wiper while the boat was under way. The boat hit an object or a wave and the skipper was thrown overboard and disappeared from sight.

The passenger, unfamiliar with the craft, was unable to get the engine turned off until the boat had travelled some distance from where the skipper went over.

We anchored the cruiser and with the two boats searched the area till after dark. Unsuccessful, we returned to the cruiser and brought the passenger to the marina.

The Ontario Provincial Police arrived and brought the cruiser into dock. The O.P.P. reported that the propeller was bent. The craft may have hit something and this might have caused the loss rather than the wave action.

The next day the search was under way. It was very difficult using the grappling irons with the amount of weed growth in the inner bay. Eight days later a fisherman came upon the body in the weeds in two feet of water.

These are two of the boating accidents which resulted in loss of life off Long Point. Lack of respect for these waters, poor seamanship, and bad judgement caused many more.

One day, while heading down the waters of the south shore in my small boat, I came upon an example of bad judgement.

About a mile offshore my crew member, Carolyn Stienstra, spotted a canoe upside down in the lake. We headed for it and found a man holding onto the overturned canoe and a small child in a lifejacket 20 feet away. Carolyn immediately reached over and pulled the crying child aboard. We then put a line on the canoe and towed it and the man to shore.

Once ashore we discovered what had happened. They were campers from the provincial park six miles down the lake. It had been a beautiful morning, the lake flat, and he had decided to run his canoe down the lakeshore, with his small son accompanying him. Not aware that the wind usually picks up at noon, they had travelled some distance down the lake using the small outboard motor on the canoe.

Shortly before we came along, the winds had picked up considerably and the lake had roughened. The winds had blown the small craft offshore, then the waves had upset it. We just happened to be there at the right time.

The canoe and motor were hidden ashore, and we took the small lad in my boat. It wasn't big enough to take more adults, so the father started walking the six miles back to camp.

In the confusion we forgot to ask his name and campsite before leaving in my boat. The youngster was still very frightened and all he could tell us was that his mother was on the beach in a red bikini. Arriving at the park, we discovered that red bikinis were the fashion that year. After checking with three women so attired, we were still unsuccessful. We walked through the park and eventually the youngster recognized his family's camper.

We left the child with his mother, and the father made it back on foot hours later.

When one sails in Long Point waters today, he should be aware that many of those sailors lost years ago were much more knowledgeable of the treacherous waters off Long Point than the modern-day weekend sailor.

Looking for a place to make an emergency landing on the south beach. Regular landings on the beach are not permitted.
— Dave Stone

Aircraft

Long Point is noted for the great number of vessels and lives that have been lost to its surrounding waters and offshore bars. No mention, however, has ever been made of the tragedies and troubles that have resulted from aircraft mishaps and pranks.

In starting this section, what would be more fitting than to mention one of the world's greatest pilots who, after his record-setting transatlantic flight, flew over Long Point.

This was none other than Colonel Charles Lindbergh. During 1930 he was visiting a friend, Mr. Harry Brook, a noted Simcoe industrialist. They decided to take a flight over Long Point and the surrounding area. A plane was rented and they made the flight. Lindbergh, a conservationist, was very impressed with the natural state of the Long Point wilderness.

One of the humorous incidents that happened with aircraft at Long Point occurred during the Second World War. Two young airmen had been doing a bit of drinking in their canteen at the R.C.A.F. Bombing and Gunnery School at Jarvis. As the spirits which they had been consuming started to work, they came up with this tremendous idea. One airman's civilian girlfriend had wanted a ride in an aircraft. After another drink or two they went into action.

The one young hero left the base, picked up his girlfriend and smuggled her into the station. The three of them then went to the airstrip, where the Anson training planes were sitting on the runway. They started one up and shortly were having a great time flying over Long Point country.

As they neared the breakwater on the south beach of Long Point, the plane started to sputter. This had a sobering effect on the pilot when he realized their peril.

There was no place to land a plane that size on the beach, so he decided to put it down in shallow water just offshore. This he did successfully, and they all climbed out on a wing and started hollering.

Nearby was a keeper's cabin belonging to the Long Point Company. The company had some of these cabins distributed over their property and manned to keep the poachers out. The keeper at the breakwater heard their hollering and headed for the beach. He couldn't believe his eyes when he saw this fair-sized aircraft just offshore on the verge of sinking, and he was startled to see two airmen in uniform and a civilian girl standing on a wing.

He got into his boat and rowed out to rescue them. Once he got them ashore, he realized that the two airmen were not suffering from shock but were still a bit intoxicated. He made arrangements to have them taken back to their base.

What happened there is unknown, but you can be sure they didn't receive love and kisses from their commanding officer. After all, what can you say after you become intoxicated, smuggle a civilian into the base, steal a plane and then sink it at Long Point?

On July 21, 1958, a tragedy occurred on the Point. Two young men, flying out of Welland, decided to fly over a cottage which was occupied by the girlfriend of one of the men. Coming in too low, the plane hit a large tree, tearing both wings off. The plane plummeted to the ground, broke into many pieces, and the engine ended up some distance from the impact, burying itself in the sand. Both men were killed instantly. The plane, totally demolished, could have been picked up in a wheelbarrow.

On a beautiful July day in 1964, hundreds of bathers, suntanners, and parents playing with their children were scattered along the ten-mile sandy beach at Long Point. Everyone was having a good time at the water's edge. Suddenly the roar of a plane engine was heard. Looking up, one could see a plane coming in at a very low level.

People started to panic, running, grabbing their children, screaming, some standing in amazement as they couldn't believe their eyes, and others dropped flat onto the sand. It was like an episode right out of World War II — a plane coming in, flying low, guns blazing, strafing hundreds of unsuspecting civilians.

As this plane dove on the beach and then levelled off, it seemed to be flying just over the heads of those still standing.

This small plane continued buzzing for 15 minutes, back and forth, covering the entire stretch of beach, resulting in utter confusion and fear for those still left scrambling to safety.

Eventually the aircraft, after its final dive, proceeded west and disappeared from sight.

After the plane disappeared, the beach looked as if a major disaster had struck: upset picnic baskets, blankets strewn everywhere, sandpails and toys scattered from one end to the other. Slowly and cautiously people started returning to the beach, others stood up and looked west, hoping the plane had disappeared once and for all.

Fortunately, several parties had recorded the numbers of the plane and the authorities were notified immediately. This information was turned over to the R.C.M.P., whose investigation reported the plane was flying out of London, Ontario. The pilot was charged and convicted of this offence, resulting in the loss of his pilot's licence.

Such a performance has not been repeated along the beach at Long Point. Planes flying over this built-up area of lakefront stay at approximately the thousand-foot level.

The first reported landing on Long Point was by pilot Earl Sandt of Pennsylvania in the winter of 1912. Sandt, flying his biplane across the lake, ran out of gas near the Point. He was fortunate that when his engine stopped he was able to glide his craft to the beach and make a safe landing. The lighthouse keeper, William Porritt, supplied fuel for Sandt, and he took off safely and returned to Erie.

Around the 1930s a plane bearing a crew of two went down in the lake. The downed plane, after being in the water a week, was located by a fishing tug out of Port Dover. The plane was lashed to the side of the tug and brought into port. After a week in the cold water, the occupants still retained their looks of life and were undisturbed even to their caps and goggles. The cockpit of the aircraft had to be cut away to remove the bodies because the sides had closed in on them as a result of the crash.

In June of 1964 another plane crash took place at the end of Long Point near the lighthouse. Killed in this tragedy were two prominent Simcoe residents, Mr. and Mrs. James Leatherdale. Mr. Leatherdale, the pilot, was well known for his numerous aerial rescue missions and was considered an excellent pilot.

The lighthouse keeper, Mr. William Ansley, said that he had seen a plane circling and realized it was in trouble, but he did not see the crash. He went to the beach, spotted the wreckage of the plane, and reported the crash by radio to the Department of Transport, Port Burwell.

The officials and rescuers had a very difficult time getting to this isolated part of the Point. Two boats travelled through rough waters, fog and darkness to try to aid the victims. Fortunately, on board one of the boats was Mr. Harvey Ferris, who knew Long Point well, having lived there all his life. He was also well known for the part he had played in many rescue missions. Dr. D.A. Archibald made it to the end of the Point by jeep.

Neither victim had survived this plane crash.

The police summarized that the pilot was attempting to crash land after the plane had stalled. It looked as if it had just slipped into the ground. With the exception of the engine the plane was a total loss.

In May 1967 a one-man Gyrocopter made a flight from Long Point to Port Rowan. It wasn't the flight that created the sensation but the way the pilot returned home after many years absence.

Albert Cudney hadn't visited Port Rowan in more than 20 years. He made a grand entrance from the sky on his three-wheeled, one-man Gyrocopter. The hometown folks were really shook up when they spotted this strange-looking craft making a landing, especially when from it stepped Albert Cudney, a former Port Rowan High School student.

The craft only weighed 200 pounds and didn't have much more than a seat, motor and a pair of helicopter blades, plus a bit of tubing.

The pilot had towed the craft behind his car from Raleigh, North Carolina, to Long Point, and from there he had launched his craft for Port Rowan.

People asked him why he did it. "I just had a desire to see my boyhood haunts from a different viewpoint," Cudney replied.

Today, when you go into Port Rowan, you'll see some of the old-timers looking up at the sky. They are looking and wondering who the next visitor from outer space is going to be.

One of the closest calls concerning aircraft ever witnessed by former lighthouse keeper Bill Ansley involved a plane going in for a landing on the north shore just south of Gravelley Bay. Seeing that it did not take off again, he and the other keeper on duty, Clayton Scofield, went down the beach several miles to check it out.

There the plane sat, on the beach near the end of a sandspit, and beside the plane stood two people. They were having difficulty keeping the engine going. Every so often it would cough, out would come a cloud of smoke and it would quit. They thought the engine was flooded.

Eventually the motor began to run smoothly and the pilot decided to take off. Instead of taking the long run down the sandspit, he decided to take the short run the other way because the wind conditions were ideal.

The plane took off from the beach, then started

Jean Stone greeting the pilot that just put his aircraft down on the waters near Ryerson Island so he could have a swim.
— Dave Stone

Coast Guard Canada supplied this hovercraft for use at the Long Point lighthouse. The lighthouse keepers found it unsatisfactory in the high seas, so it was not used at the station.

coming down to the lake. The plane just seemed to hover above the water with the wheels now and then touching the surface.

Both lighthouse keepers on shore were certain they were about to witness a terrible plane crash and the loss of two lives. Fortunately, this did not happen, as the plane started to lift. It continued climbing and soon disappeared from view.

The two keepers returned to their station still not believing what they had just witnessed.

My first plane trip to the lighthouse was a very memorable occasion. I had made the trip hundreds of times by boat, but this plane trip stands out more than any of them. It happened this way.

One early spring day in 1964 I ran into my friend George Backus in Port Rowan. George, who was in the lumber and building business, asked me if I would like to go to the end of the Point with him. He was building a new cement-block fog alarm building at the

lighthouse and was going out there to see how the job was progressing.

In those days I didn't know George was an excellent pilot and owned his own aircraft, so I thought this trip would be made by driving on the beach in a jeep to the lighthouse. We got in George's truck and headed for St. Williams. I couldn't figure this out because we were going the wrong way.

George parked the truck just at the edge of the village. Over the fence we went, through a muddy field to a small metal building. I rounded the building to the open side, and there was a small plane. I looked at the plane and then the soft muddy field and started to wonder what I was doing there.

We pushed the plane out of the hangar and gassed up. George was as cool as a cucumber, but I was uptight. George checked the plane all over, and I noticed he had something in his hands. He told me they were mousetraps that he had just taken out of

Transport Canada's helicopter bringing in a change of crew and supplies to the lighthouse.
— Dave Stone

some openings in the wings. These are placed in the plane when it is sitting in the hangar because mice eat the dope in the fabric and this weakens the strength of the material. This bit of information nearly threw me, but I gritted my teeth and prepared myself.

We both climbed in. George let the engine run for a while, then gave it the throttle and down the field we went. I was sure we would never get off that soft field.

However, this was no problem for George. We took off smoothly and headed for the lighthouse. I settled down and started to enjoy viewing Long Point from the air.

There was a nice stretch of beach near the lighthouse and we came in for a landing. Just as we neared our approach, I spotted a large box right in our path. I knew this was it. But not George, he just eased the plane up, and then onto the beach we came, with not so much as a bump. I realized then what a privilege it was for me to be flying with a real pro and my fears left me completely.

Since that day I have made a number of flights with George and they have all been most enjoyable. But why not when I'm flying with one of the best!

Aircraft carry on very important functions on Long Point. Frequently the Coast Guard Canada helicopter can be seen travelling back and forth from Prescott to the lighthouse with supplies, equipment, or lightkeepers who are making a shift change.

The Ontario Provincial Police helicopter and the large Hercules from the armed services base at Trenton also fly search missions for downed planes, missing hunters and fishermen, or boats in distress or lost. On numerous occasions these aircraft have been used to find missing persons and have been successful. They are all to be congratulated for the excellent service they have rendered. Without them the total of lives lost on the Point would be much greater.

In this section I have tried to show that the fickle Point's clutching sands are still taking unwary victims. Novices and experienced pilots alike have made Long Point their "Last Port of Call," the same as it was in years gone by when both inexperienced and veteran sailors were lost to the Point's whims.

A famous ship out of the past sails around Long Point.
— Jack Southcott

"The Bounty"

On July 27, 1986, the salmon fishermen off Long Point couldn't believe their eyes. Coming up in their midst was the beautiful replica of H.M.S. *Bounty*. Rounding the Point, she sailed up the lake for stops at various ports.

Bounty was built in Lunenburg for the movie production of *The Bounty*. This film tells the story of the mutiny aboard the ship in 1797.

She is one of the last wooden square-riggers. They aren't building them anymore because shipwrights and their skills are fast disappearing.

The original *Bounty* was less than five years old when mutineer Christian stripped and burned her, leaving no trace, so they couldn't be spotted by the British navy off Pitcairn Island, where they had settled.

The *Bounty* was 47 metres long and weighed 500 tonnes. Her main mast towered 31 metres above the deck. She carried 90 square metres of sail and 20 kilometres of rope.

When I first became interested in the shipwrecks off Long Point, I imagined them sitting upright in crystal clear water with a valuable cargo on board. Like most researchers starting on this quest, my dreams were no different than those of my fellow divers. But my dreams of finding a fortune slowly faded away when the fact was accepted that this was Long Point, Lake Erie, not the Spanish Main.

I have found no great monetary treasures on or off Long Point, but I have discovered treasure and been rewarded immeasurably.

Many years have passed since I first stumbled onto a wreck on the beach. It was on that my treasures and rewards started to accumulate. A learning experience concerning Long Point had started which, a number of years later, I would be able to share with all those who were interested. I have learned much of the folklore and nature of the Point from many of the old keepers of the Long Point Company. The lighthouse keepers have shared stories that would fill volumes about happenings at the tip. I have experienced being at the lighthouse at midnight under a full moon, watching the beacons casting their beams approximately 25 miles over the water. I have listened to the foghorn sound for two days straight, warning those offshore of the impending dangers nearby, the whole area closed in with fog, the lake invisible from shore. Having experienced being on this wind-swept beach, miles from civilization during a violent storm, I can visualize a ship aground on a bar and the crew trying to make it ashore in the pounding surf.

Another reward has been the exploration of the remains of shipwrecks lying on the bottom of the lake. A shipwreck to me is not just a pile of old boards, but a time capsule. My imagination runs wild!

Getting to know Long Point's entire physical structure, from the base to the tip, has also been very gratifying.

I have been involved with nearly all that has happened at Long Point during my lifetime, and touched remains of lifetimes passed.

I have met many divers, naturalists, museum curators, archaeologists, biologists, geologists, bird watchers, shipwreck researchers, lighthouse keepers, Ministry of Natural Resources staff, Canadian Wildlife Service staff, marine archaeologists, historians, commercial fishermen, and laymen who have accumulated a great deal of information about Long Point. All the above have shared their knowledge with me. What a chestful of gems I have received from these people!

Now for the big payoff, which is worth all the treasure lying at the bottom of Lake Erie. As a direct result of my intense interest in Long Point and its shipwrecks, two young people had the course of their lives changed. Both spent their growing years as part of my crew, both became divers and fell in love with the water.

Carolyn Stienstra, a Long Point neighbour's daughter, started going out with me in the boat when she was eight years old. She spent her summers on Long Point from then until she graduated from high school. She became a very efficient first mate. During her time with me she became a diver and we shared some wreck diving experiences together. The die was now well cast

Former crew member Carolyn Stienstra, officer in the Canadian Coast Guard.

for her future. It had to be something to do with the sea. She enrolled in the Canadian Coast Guard College and became an officer. Since graduation she has served on a number of Coast Guard ships based out of Dartmouth, Nova Scotia. She also married an officer in the Navy.

Heath Stone, my son, spent his growing years either in his or my boat in the waters of Long Point. He became as familiar as I with every nook and cranny on Long Point. Not only was he interested in shipwrecks, but all the "little critters" that lived on the bottom. He also became a diver. Once out of high school he went to university and end up with several degrees in marine biology. Today he is a marine biologist consultant in Dartmouth, Nova Scotia.

To those who cherish this place called Long Point, with its miles of wilderness, ponds, creeks, wetlands, dunes and forests, its surrounding waters covering shipwreck disasters of long ago, may these pages rekindle the obsession for this place where land and water meet.

Former crew member, Heath Stone, marine biologist.

If you are unfamiliar with the graveyard of the Great Lakes, let this be a beginning, a spark of interest for this phenomenon of nature.

Long Point has been my life's endeavour, and through these stories I share my treasure with you.

Bibliography

Andrews, Captain W.D. *The Lifeboat*. Toronto: William Briggs, 1890

Ballenge, Jack M. "Lake Erie Graveyard." *Skin Diver*, 1944.

Bannister, Dr. John A. *Long Point and Its Lighthouses*. Lawson Memorial Library, University of Western Ontario, London, Ontario.

Barrett, Harry B. *Lore and Legends of Long Point*. Don Mills, Ontario: Burns & MacEachern Limited, 1977.

Berman, Bruce D. *Encyclopedia of American Shipwrecks*. Boston: Mariners Press Incorporated, 1973.

Blythe, Chris A. "A Lake Erie Dive Site." *The Canadian Diver News*.

Bowen, Dana Thomas. *Lore of the Lakes*. Cleveland: Freshwater Press Incorporated, 1940.

Bowen, Dana Thomas. *Memories of the Lakes*. Cleveland: Freshwater Press Incorporated, 1946.

Bowen, Dana Thomas. *Shipwrecks of the Lakes*. Freshwater Press Incorporated, 1952.

Boyer, Dwight. *Great Stories of the Great Lakes*. New York: Dodd, Mead and Company, 1966.

Boyer, Dwight. *Ghost Ships of the Great Lakes*. New York: Dodd, Mead and Company, 1968.

Boyer, Dwight. *True Tales of the Great Lakes*. New York: Dodd, Mead and Company, 1971.

Collins, Bob and Bob Mann. "The Night the Whisky Ship Went Aground." *Macleans Magazine*, September 15, 1958.

Doner, Mary Frances. *The Salvager*. Minneapolis: Ross and Haines Incorporated, 1958.

Dickerson, T.A. *A Review of Shipwrecks on Long Point, Ontario, 1827-1959*.

Fox, William A. *The Culture History of Long Point*. London, 1985.

Gordon, W.A. and John. *Lake Erie's Isle of Romance*. Port Dover, Ontario: The Photo Print Shop, 1934.

Harrison, John MacLean. *The Fate of the Griffon*. Griffin Press Limited, 1974.

Heden, Karl E. *Directory of Shipwrecks of the Great Lakes*. Boston: Bruce Humphries, 1966.

Inland Seas, A Quarterly Journal of the Great Lakes Historical Society. Vermillion, Ohio.

Knister, R. "Long Point, Lake Erie." *Canadian Geographical Journal*, 1931.

Laider, George. "Long Point, Lake Erie: Some Physical and Historical Aspects." Ontario Historical Society.

Lonsdale, Adrian L. and H.R. Kaplan. *A Guide to Sunken Ships in American Waters*. Arlington, Virginia: Compass Publications Incorporated, 1964.

Mansfield, J.B. *History of the Great Lakes*. Chicago: J.H. Beer & Company, 1899.

Norfolklore, Publications of the Norfolk Historical Society, Simcoe, Ontario.

Ministry of Transport. "Statement of Shipping Casualties Resulting in Total Loss on Inland Waters Exceeding the St. Lawrence River Below Montreal From 1870 to 1976." Compiled by Captain W.A.W. Catinus.

Pearce, Bruce M. *Historical Highlights of Norfolk County*. Hamilton, Ontario: Griffin and Richmond Company Ltd., 1973.

Public Archives Ontario. List of Ships Employed on British Naval Service on the Great Lakes 1755 to 1875. K. MacPherson.

Public Archives Canada. "Loss of Life and Property on Lake Erie on the Canadian Coast 1858-68."

Ratigan, William. *Great Lakes Shipwrecks and Survivals*. New York: William B. Eerdmans Publishing Company, 1960.

Tait, Lyal. *The Petuns, Tobacco Indians of Canada*. Port Burwell, Ontario: Erie Publishers, 1971.

Seasons, Special Issue on Long Point. *The Nature and Outdoor Magazine*, Spring 1981.

U.S. Government Treasury Department, United States Lifesaving Service, 1881.

NEWSPAPERS

Cleveland *Plain Dealer*, Cleveland, Ohio.
Delhi *News Record*, Delhi, Ontario.
Simcoe *Reformer*, Simcoe, Ontario.
Hamilton *Spectator*, Hamilton, Ontario.
Huron *Church News*, London, Ontario.
London *Free Press*, London, Ontario.
Nanticoke *Times*, Waterford, Ontario.
Port Dover *Maple Leaf*, Port Dover, Ontario.

OTHER RESEARCH

Eva Brook Donly Museum, Simcoe, Ontario.
Great Lakes Historical Society, Vermillion, Ohio.
Institute for Great Lakes Research, Bowling Green State University, Bowling Green, Ohio.
Public Archives, Ottawa, Ontario.
Public Archives, Toronto, Ontario.
Toronto Mariner Historical Society, Toronto, Ontario.
University of Western Ontario, London, Ontario.

Seagulls are shipwrecked sailors returning home.

— *Dave Stone*

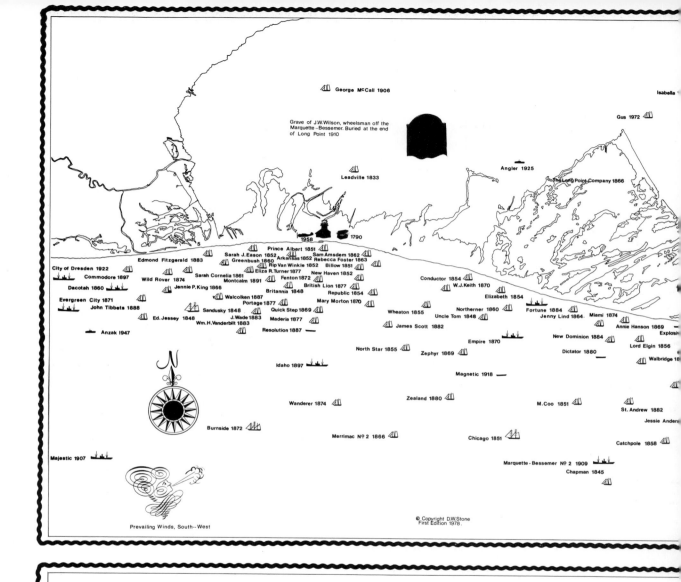

RECORDED SHIPWRECKS SINCE THE 18TH. CENTURY
ON AND OFF LONG POINT, ONTARIO.

RESEARCH AND PRODUCTION BY D.W.STONE
"The Beachcomber of Long Point"
ARTIST AND CARTOGRAPHER, K.W.HAWKINS.

OCT 1, 1986
Dan Stone
THE BEACHCOMBER OF LONG POINT

THE GHOST FLEET OF L
Graveyard of the Grea

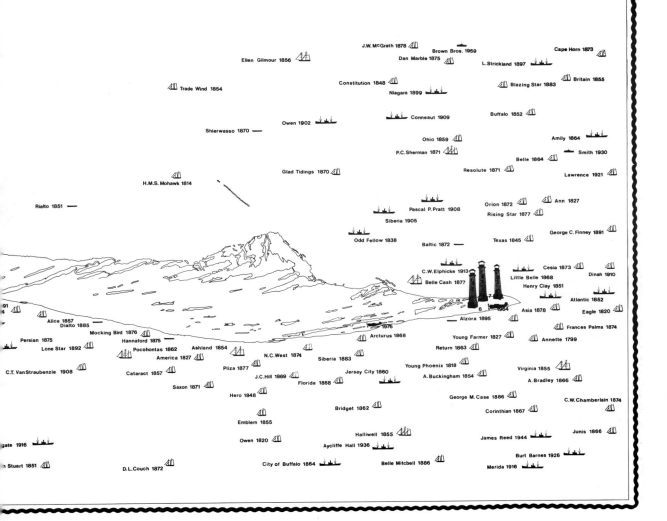

J.W. McGrath 1878
Brown Bros. 1959
Cape Horn 1873
Ellen Gilmour 1856
Dan Marble 1875
L. Strickland 1897
Constitution 1848
Blazing Star 1883
Britain 1855
Trade Wind 1854
Niagara 1899
Owen 1902
Conneaut 1909
Buffalo 1852
Shierwasso 1870
Ohio 1859
Amily 1864
P.C. Sherman 1871
Smith 1930
Belle 1864
Glad Tidings 1870
Resolute 1871
Lawrence 1921
H.M.S. Mohawk 1814
Rialto 1851
Pascal P. Pratt 1908
Orion 1872
Ann 1827
Siberia 1905
Rising Star 1877
George C. Finney 1891
Odd Fellow 1838
Baltic 1872
Texas 1845
C.W. Elphicke 1913
Cesia 1873
Dinah 1910
Belle Cash 1877
Little Belle 1868
Henry Clay 1851
Atlantic 1852
Asia 1878
Eagle 1820
Alice 1857
Alzora 1895
Frances Palms 1874
Dialto 1885
Mocking Bird 1876
Young Farmer 1827
Annette 1799
Persian 1875
Return 1863
Lone Star 1892
Pocohontas 1862
Ashland 1854
Virginia 1855
America 1827
N.C. West 1874
Siberia 1883
A. Bradley 1866
C.T. VanStraubenzie 1908
Pliza 1877
Young Phoenix 1818
Cataract 1857
J.C. Hill 1869
Jersey City 1860
A. Buckingham 1854
Saxon 1871
Florida 1868
George M. Case 1886
C.W. Chamberlain 1874
Hero 1848
Bridget 1862
Corinthian 1867
Emblem 1855
gate 1916
Halliwell 1855
James Reed 1944
Junis 1866
Owen 1820
Aycliffe Hall 1936
Burt Barnes 1926
Stuart 1851
City of Buffalo 1864
Belle Mitchell 1886
Merida 1916
D.L. Couch 1872

POINT
kes

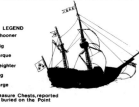

LEGEND
Schooner
Brig
Barque
Freighter
Tug
Barge
Treasure Chests, reported
buried on the Point
Airplane crashes

THE BARQUE GRIFFON
The first ship to narrowly miss disaster on Long Point
Robert Cavalier De La Salle's barque Le Griffon, westbound, was the first ship to sail past Long Point in 1679. A smothering fog was hugging the surface when a sailor reported the soundings had suddenly lessened to three fathoms. Awaiting the lifting of the brune, the famed "Voyageur" found the low sand cape of Long Point stretched out before him. Thankful for having been spared the fate of so many later mariners, he christened the strip "Point Saint Francois."

LIGHTHOUSES
1   1830 – 1843 Washed out
2   1843 – 1915 Washed out – burned 1929
3   1915 Still operating
4   1879 – 1916 Still standing – not in use
LIFESAVING STATIONS
5   1883 – 1911
6   1911 – 1912
7   1912 – 1926

ABOUT THE BOOK

It is hard to imagine when cruising the waters off Long Point, Ontario, on a beautiful summer's day, that one is travelling in an area known as the "graveyard" of the Great Lakes. This body of water has for over two centuries taken a vast toll of lives, ships and cargoes. *Long Point: Last Port of Call* tells the story of a number of these shipwreck disasters that occurred off this treacherous sandspit.

With the frequency of Marine losses, especially during the days of sail and early steam, stories are told of the establishment of Long Point's lighthouses and lifesaving station. This book is not only an account of marine catastrophes but of other adventures as well pertaining to Long Point. Humorous anecdotes by the author and other Long Point characters add to the richness of these stories told about *Long Point: Last Port of Call*.

ABOUT THE AUTHOR

Dave Stone has been intimately involved with Long Point and its shipwrecks for over 35 years. As an experienced diver, not only has he researched these wrecks, but he has visited them in their watery graves.

He was raised in the town of Ingersoll and during his early years spent summers at Turkey Point, where his fascination for Long Point began.

During the war he was in the Royal Canadian Navy on Atlantic convoy. He was a member of the crew of the corvette H.M.C.S. *Chilliwack*, which took part in the longest submarine hunt in the history of the Canadian Navy, resulting in the capture and destruction of the U774 on March 5 and 6, 1944.

Over the years he has shared his knowledge of Long Point through numerous slide presentations, TV documentaries, published articles and his shipwreck chart, "The Ghost Fleet of Long Point."

Dave and his wife, Jean, reside in Ingersoll and Long Point. They have two children, Julia and Heath. Throughout the Long Point area he is known as "The Beachcomber of Long Point".